An Eden of Sorts

An Eden of Sorts

The Natural History
of My Feral Garden

❋❋❋

John Hanson Mitchell

Countryman Press
Woodstock, Vermont

Library of Congress Cataloging-in-Publication Data have been applied for.

An Eden of Sorts

978-1-58157-172-1

Paintings © by Suzan Osborn
Book design and composition by S. E. Livingston

Published by The Countryman Press, P.O. Box 748, Woodstock, VT 05091

Distributed by W. W. Norton & Company, Inc., 500 Fifth Avenue, New York, NY 10110

Printed in China

10 9 8 7 6 5 4 3 2 1

For Clayton, Lelia, Alex, Gabriel, Avery, Kai,
Maya, Wyatt, and those to come.

1236

AN EDEN OF SORTS

ACKNOWLEDGMENTS

This type of project, involving nearly thirty years of efforts of various sorts, acquires a huge number of colleagues, sources, contributors, and assistants, some of whom may not have realized they were giving me information that would later appear in print. Many of these were contributors to *Sanctuary* magazine, the journal of the Massachusetts Audubon Society, which I edited for over thirty years. These writers, plus the staff at the society, were invaluable providers of information on a variety of sometimes arcane matters, such as the identification of mosses and lichens, the local effects of global climate change on blooming times, land-preservation strategies, the mating habits of salamanders and dragonflies, and, of course, the changing trends in bird populations over the last thirty years.

Prime among these contributors were past and present members of the Mass Audubon staff, including, in no particular order, Chris Leahy, Wayne Petersen, Simon Perkins, Tom Tyning, Robie Hubley, Betsy Colburn, Skip Lazell, Joe Choiniere, Jim Baird, Dan Hart, and my mentor in these matters, the now deceased curmudgeonly journalist known as Mr. Hanley.

The regular writers for *Sanctuary* also provided me with a wealth of information. These include Tom Conuel, Gayle Goddard-Taylor, Michael Caduto, Teri Chace, Nini Bloch, Ann Prince, Brian Donahue, David Foster, Karl Meyer, David Gessner, Bill Scheller, Tom Wessels, and many others who, during my tenure as editor, wrote a story or two and then moved on.

By far the greatest number of sources were those various authorities or amateurs on landscape preservation, gardening, field biology, painting and writing, and especially those who, over the years, have given me cast-off perennials and trees and shrubs from their own gardens. I also had encouragement from those many gardeners and non-gardeners alike who only admired my handiwork. These include, again in no particular order, Whit Beals, Joy Reo, Ron MacAdow, Lawrence Millman, Alice Moro, Jaceck Basita, Abigail Higgins, Susan Schnare, Rick Findlay, Dori Smith, Richard Forman, Suzan Osborn, Jill Brown, Susie Singer, Moragh Ramage, Madeleine Findlay, Eva Apfelbaum, Diane Winkleman, Kim and Larry Buel, Jane Chrisfield, Peter Mitchell, Merloyd Lawrence, and the unidentified ladies of numerous garden-club tours. Furthermore, I had a number of volunteer gardeners who have helped me out over the years, including my two brothers, James and Hugh, and my nephews Peter and Jim, and finally, my son-in-law, Captain Good Boy, aka Jason Leary, who first earned his place in this ongoing project by helping me transport and plant trees.

I would also like to thank the children of the garden, who, although they did not know it, taught me to see, and to whom this book is dedicated.

CONTENTS

I seem to have wandered into a land of greater fertility,
some up-country Eden.

✺ HENRY DAVID THOREAU

PREFACE

The Vicarage Garden

Some years ago I moved onto an acre-and-a-half plot of earth in a region of low, rolling hills dotted with extensive forests, a few farms and orchards, and a developing suburban area to the east, toward the city. This was by no means a spectacular piece of property. It was originally an apple orchard that stretched from the marshes of a brook to the east, westward over a low hill to a level agricultural area known locally as Scratch Flat, a tract of land that had been in cultivation for over a thousand years, if you include Native American history. The apple orchard was cut down in the 1920s to make a horse pasture, and after the horses died and the family moved west, the property had grown up to white pines.

On the west side of the hill, beyond the forest, there were two working farms, and just across the road to the east there was another farm, this one abandoned and characterized by a series of overgrown pastures that dropped down to the slow, north-running stream with a wide floodplain of cattail marshes.

The pine forest was a dark, foreboding place. The thick canopy shut out all hint of sunlight, and the forest floor was open and devoid of a shrub layer. In an unofficial inventory of the tract, I once counted a mere five species of higher plants there—poison ivy, starflower, sarsaparilla, partridgeberry, and three ancient apple trees, left over from the time when the land was all orchard. I identified three or four species of mushrooms, a few mosses, and three types of lichens. Blue jays flew through the forest from time to time; a great horned owl would alight there occasionally, and flycatchers used to perch at the edge of the woods. But as far as I could tell, no birds actually nested there. Mammals such as foxes and coyotes passed through, and there must have been a number of mice. But the only evidence of mammal habitation I ever found was a gray-squirrel nest.

What I really wanted on this land, or at least what I imagined I wanted, was a flowering mead and a sunny garden where dragonflies crisscrossed and crickets sang all summer long, someplace where you could walk in spring over the fresh green shoots of emerging grasses or lie on your back in autumn and watch the speedy dragonflies dart by and the slow drift of migrating hawks.

With this in mind, and not without a certain amount of internal debate, I finally decided to undertake that anathema of environmentalists, a clear-cut, and remake the whole property. With the help of an environmentally benign team of mules—as opposed to a ground-ripping skidder—I had the entire section of the forest cut, and over the course of the next two years created a semblance of a meadow. Not quite what I had in mind—there were more weeds than grasses there—but at least I had a clear view of the sky and the sun.

The cleared land, along with a grove of hickory trees on the northwestern corner of the property, seemed to invite more shaping—some sort of definition to fix the open space in the midst of the generally wooded landscape that surrounded the property. As it was, I found myself spending more and more time there, thinking out the roll of the land, the angles of the walls, and the blank slate of the meadow. After a few years, I built a small Thoreauvian-style cottage in the hickory grove and settled in. Because I mounted a carved ornamental swan above the front door, the place became known as the Swan Cottage.

I lived there for two years, not unlike my hero, Henry Thoreau, save that Henry went to the woods so that he could live deliberately. I originally moved to the cottage because I was splitting up with my wife and needed a place to stay.

Suffice to say this separation was not so much of a break in the typical American style. It was more like a marital split among certain tribal cultures in which couples who divorce simply build a new hut nearby for one of the partners. Children are shared by various parents and stepparents, grandparents, aunts and uncles. In our case, we legally divided the property and I simply moved up the hill away from my old house and its hard-won surround of flower beds and vegetable gardens and started all over.

There were other marked differences from Henry Thoreau's Walden experience. Rather than a pond and a grove of arrowy pines and a bean field, not half a mile away from my land there was a major highway. Furthermore, the year I built my modest dwelling, a computer company constructed a vast empire of low-slung buildings and parking lots in a formerly thriving pear orchard, thereby destroying forever the generally rural character of the town center.

Nevertheless, in the face of the declining local environment—in fact in some ways because of the decline—as soon as I moved in I began planting new gardens. I laid out a long narrow plot along the west wall, and planted it with vegetables and annuals and a couple of pear trees. Even so, the little clearing seemed to cry out for more, some larger statement that would fix this otherwise indistinct plot of earth as a place.

It was during this period that, for no very good reason, I turned down an intriguing story assignment to cover the huge Krishna Festival in Mathura, India. I had come to realize by then that, along with Mole of *The Wind in the Willows* fame, I was an animal of the plowed furrow and hedgerow, more tied to my own grounds. The story assignment was for midsummer, and there was no place on earth that I would rather be in midsummer than cultivating my own gardens. With this revelation, I decided that I should go ahead and build a real house on the land.

I had long been interested in the work of the nineteenth-century garden designer and architect Andrew Jackson Downing. I appreciated his romantic, wild versions of British and European garden designs, as well as his house plans. After much wrangling over permits and the architectural variances that, in our unimaginative era, were required in order to accomplish Downing's brave designs, I constructed another house on the property, in the Carpenter Gothic style. The place was set on a rise above a long curving drive that ran along an old stone wall on the north side of the tract.

Once I moved into the house, I began designing, step by step and accident by accident, a series of garden rooms based on Downing's plans, coupled with a few flourishes gleaned from the garden writings of Edith Wharton, as well as a few Italian villa gardens that had been designed by English gardeners in the early nineteenth century. Finally, after a period of five or six years, the grounds began to take shape.

I planted a mix of flowering trees and shrubs along the north wall that bordered the driveway. On the south side of the drive, I put in an island of trees I called the Bishop's Close, named after a fine garden at a former rectory property turned garden between Lake Oswego and Portland, Oregon. I put in a bank of flower beds in front of the entrance door, in the style of a French peasant cottage, and at the head of the drive, I laid out a grassy allée bordered by a shrub mix, leading to a nineteenth-century garden shed I salvaged from a nearby property. And behind the house, around the little Thoreauvian cottage I had lived in, I expanded the vegetable and flower gardens along the back wall.

The main garden lay on the south side of the house. Here, after many designs and redesigns, I created what was known by French garden designers as a *patte d'oie*, or goose foot—a semicircle of lawn, with five allées leading off to a series of garden rooms. At the end of the central path I built a little summer house, along with more vegetable and flower gardens, a mini orchard to the southwest, and to the southeast, a hedge maze, copied from a labyrinth design I had seen in the floor of the basilica in Ravenna, Italy.

All through this landscape, and all around the house, and beside the wall along the road, and also by the side of another privet allée leading up to the house from the road, I planted, among the existing hickories and maples, many varieties of ornamental trees and shrubs, and when all that was done, I began to look around for more spaces to fill.

In short, I seemed to suffer from a bad case of what an English visitor to these grounds used to call *horror vacuui*, an art term referring to the apparent need of Late Baroque artists to fill in absolutely every available space on a canvas.

In the end, what emerged from all this digging and delving was a half-formal, half-uncared-for wild garden that resembled in some ways a semiformal Italian garden, in some ways a romantic design out of Andrew Jackson Downing's book *Victorian Cottage Residences*, plus a few of my own follies of design, such as a circle of ornamental trees termed *le bosque sacré*.

I have an English gardening friend from Royal Tunbridge Wells in Kent, a woman of a certain age, who visits regularly during the growing season. Mrs. Theodosia Huntingfield, better known locally as the English Lady, is not averse to expressing her opinions on my garden follies. On one of her early visits I described to her my various influences, such as the Villa Cimbrone, in Ravello, the gardens at Villa La Pietra, in Florence, and my hero Andrew Jackson Downing. She looked up along the flowering mead to the house, with its surround of dark pointed trees and the gabled roofline and the stained-glass Palladian front window.

"More like a vicarage garden, if you ask me," she said.

Which, quite by accident, and in spite of the fact that there is no church anywhere nearby, nor any vicar, I suppose it is. In fact, one of my, probably unconscious, models for this folly is the vicarage garden of my other hero in these matters, the great eighteenth-century naturalist Gilbert White, author of *The Natural History and Antiquities of Selborne*.

❊❊❊❊❊

After a few years, this little experiment, which started as a temporary solution to a housing problem, began to assume the status of a theater set for a comedy of errors or a French farce. In time I remarried, thereby doubling the number of children on the property. My former wife remarried, and at one point sold a house she had inherited and, in order to protect herself from an encroaching housing development, bought two more adjacent lots, thus tripling the amount of property she held. In time the various children grew up, and one of them, a daughter, married and built a house on a plot of land just to the north, thus increasing the holdings of these two loosely joined families. She had two children, raising twofold the local child population. A son moved to the West Coast, married, and had a son who visited regularly throughout his babyhood and spent part of his summers in the garden. Various family members—including, in this harmonious, egalitarian group, ex partners—would come to visit, sometimes bringing children and family members from their own newly formed families. And a former nanny, not much older than her charges, adopted our families and was a regular member of any celebrations and dinner parties, as well as an occasional design strategist and gardener. Holidays evolved into major assemblages, with doddering old uncles from distant marriages drowsing by the fire, ancient great grannies and aunties, exes of my wife's family, and their children, and on and on, in what came to be known locally as "the compound."

I learned later that there was a more concise term for this living arrangement in Haitian patois—a *ladou*. The word describes a plot of land where members of a loosely extended family have settled. As I understand it, in the frequent periods of political turmoil on the island, this basic system remained more self-sufficient and stable than the country as a whole.

Also living on this *ladou* for a period of more than fifteen years were three domesticated animals, two cats and a dog, and a flock of chickens belonging to my former wife.

Thinking over the natural evolution of this landscape, it occurred to me that these domestic animals were also players in the larger story of the land. They were brought here, housed and fed, and set free to roam, and in the process they too set up a compound or territory of their own, one with a decidedly different landscape, which I have no way of actually comprehending. The smells, the sights, the sounds, were sometimes recognizable to me, but more often they were not, especially in the world of odors. I would sometimes see either the dog, or one of the cats, nose in the air, exploring in detail some invisible landscape.

As with the human family, they too had a social order of sorts, and certain defined personalities. The dog, a Jack Russell terrier who came along with my wife, was the primary defender of the compound, alert to the invasions of other species (although hardly a guard dog—he welcomed virtually all human beings, criminals and allies alike, without suspicion.) The two cats were there first, and there developed between these two alien species a certain guarded interrelationship. One of the cats was a gentle soul, a friendly, accepting individual, so kind, and so warm, that some visiting Buddhist scholars thought he might be a bodhisattva—

a perfect being, having returned to earth from Nirvana to teach we unenlightened souls the art of acceptance. He soon befriended the dog.

The other cat was more like Attila the Hun. His archenemy was the dog, who, after one encounter, chose to ignore this hissing upstart. Attila so despised the dog that in his long life (he outlived all the other animals) he never gave up his hatred and would swat the dog whenever he happened to pass within striking range.

But all that is merely the domestic side of this story. The more enduring lesson, and the great irony of the history of the garden, is the tale of what happened to this plot of earth after the native white pines were cleared.

This book is an account of the plants and animals that moved into the Vicarage Garden after I cleared the land. As will become clear, in contrast to the pine woods, this roughly two-acre patch of earth evolved into what Captain John Smith termed "an Eden of sorts" when he first saw the landscape around Boston Harbor. The garden was a dense, richly diverse habitat that supported populations of birds and butterflies, bees, dragonflies, spiders, frogs and toads, salamanders, snakes, mice, chipmunks, three species of squirrel, and even large mammals, such as fishers, foxes, deer, and bobcats—and all of this no more than thirty-five miles away from a major urban center.

The existence of grounds of this sort, so close to a city, has a long and honorable lineage. Landscape historians have speculated that the legend of the Garden of Eden may have evolved from early Sumerian enclosures located just outside city gates, in cultivated, walled plots, planted with fruiting trees and meadows and watered with streams, pools, and fountains. Here resident, half-tamed birds and mammals fed, and here the nobility spent the hot summers, cooling themselves with sherbets and the sounds of falling waters.

If that is the case, the Vicarage Garden, and in fact all gardens, even those that religiously use only native and local species, are essentially artificial environments, cultivated and clipped, and often replanted every year.

But given the opportunity, and the proper semblance of a wild habitat, and enough food sources, local wildlife will eventually make itself at home in these managed landscapes. Such was the case with the Vicarage Garden.

I.

Scratch Flat

. . . he was an animal of tilled field and hedgerow, linked to the ploughed furrow, the frequented pasture, the lane of evening lingering, the cultivated garden plot.

❋ Kenneth Graham,
The Wind in the Willows

It came to pass some years ago that one of the cousins in this extended family chose to have her wedding in the aforesaid Vicarage Garden. This begat, starting in September of the year before the wedding, a mad dash through the course of the year to clean up, replant, prune, and clear more garden rooms and paths, and dig out new flower beds in preparation for the big event.

What we had hoped to achieve that year was a greener garden, trees un-beaten down by winter snows, beds flush with flowers, borders of blooming shrubs and roses, and a normal spring. What we got was the usual. That winter, heavy snows broke branches and shrubs and folded over the boxwoods in spite of the fact that I tie them up each year. Spring was cold, a long-delayed dogwood winter, which is to say, winter in spring and snow in April. The summer of the wedding, by contrast, began with a healthy period of night rains and sun-warmed days, and all looked well for the late-summer wedding until it stopped raining at the end of June. We watered. We deadheaded annuals, and we nursed along new plantings of perennials and flowering trees, and finally, with all the work, and the clipping and mowing, and successful replanting, things looked auspicious.

But there were problems other than the capricious weather. Starting in the autumn the year before the wedding, in spite of the happy upcoming event and the garden improvements, out in the real world beyond the garden walls, things were falling apart. The great tide of the stock market receded and rose, and then fell back again to record lows. Whole fortunes were lost, banks failed, investors fled for safe ground and found nothing, stocks and bonds ebbed again and slipped seaward, and even the safe islands of money markets eroded away. Then on October 10th, the same day that the juncos arrived in the garden, I noticed that the golden hope of hedge funds fell in a steep, rushing waterfall. All the fast money that defined the recent gilded age of high finance ebbed offshore into the indifferent sea. Stocks followed suit and plunged again.

Not that any of this mattered to the garden. In late September, I went out one morning and saw a great river of gabbling black-birds flowing over the fields and gardens of Scratch Flat, just as they have every year at this time for the past two or three thousand years. Frost had come late that year, the roses were still bloom-ing in the gardens in early October; everywhere in thickets and field edges little flitting bands of Savannah sparrows appeared and disappeared, and as I often do, I hauled a chair over to a sunny corner along the western wall of my property and fell asleep in the warm light, dozing with the sound of wind, the last songs of the meadow crickets, and the cries of jays and crows all around me in the upper air.

I went out later in the week and planted tulips and daffodils and put in two new inkberries in the back garden near a sunny bench. I smelled a fox and nannyberry that day, and over on the north side of the property, from a little hollow in an oak tree, I heard the singular, bird-like chirp of a gray tree frog—the last frog of summer.

There was a green frog in my fishpond that autumn, a new frog that replaced an old bullfrog named William, who spent three summers there and then left one rainy night in early September. Spring peepers had been calling earlier that week and one day I began to see monarch butterflies passing over the flower beds. The little red meadowhawks, a species of dragonfly that shows up each year in autumn, were everywhere over the garden, alighting on the withering tomato plants, sunning themselves on the remnant flower stakes where late the last cosmos bloomed. One of the dragonflies landed on my hand while I sat dully in the garden in my place beside the wall, half-dreaming of the past summer and things to come.

A few days later, the market surged. Like ravenous dogs, buyers rushed in and it rose higher. Then the treasury secretary said something that brokers didn't want to hear. The tide fell.

I noticed the next day that the euro began to fall. Federal treasury bonds fell too, not a bad sign if you happen to have treasury bonds, I was told. The euro fell again the following day, and then again the day after that. It occurred to me that if things continued in this way I might be able to afford to get back to the gardens at Villa Lante in Italy, a place I had been thinking about for some time now. Then I met a financial adviser at a party. He told me that it is not necessarily a good thing when the euro falls. I've forgotten just why. "Don't invest in international stocks," he warned.

I told him I would not do that.

One morning in September, lounging at the table after an al fresco breakfast, I caught a glimpse of something in the woods to the northwest and saw an otter emerge into the open garden. Once in the clear, it sped through the yard toward the marshes of the nearby Beaver Brook, with that curious humping gait that otters use on dry land. I thought it was a fitting symbol. According to local Native American lore, the otter is the winter-bringer.

Robins were everywhere on the north side of Scratch Flat. Every morning, I walked out in the garden and they would be flocking and feeding in the autumn olives, an invasive shrub I had yet to clear from my land. They chattered and clucked and crossed from one wooded patch to another between my land and the neighbors' gardens.

On a warm sunny Saturday in mid-month I saw green darner dragonflies passing over the gardens, right on schedule. They're migratory, like the monarchs, and move through with clocklike regularity: Green darners on the 12th of October. Monarchs around the 5th. The blackbird flocks anywhere between the 10th and the 20th. The last of the meadow crickets around the end of the month. You could almost tell the dates by these little comings and goings.

And so it goes. Year after year, over the past three decades as I have worked to create this little oasis, the world has chugged on. Markets rose and fell. There were wars, and rumors of wars, catastrophic earthquakes, volcanoes, mudslides, and one year, I remember, there were reports that the end of the industrialized world was nigh because of some minor computer glitch that was going to happen on January 1st, 2000. But toward the end of that January I heard the mating caterwauls of the great horned owls that nest in the hemlock grove behind my garden.

Nothing changed. Nothing stayed the same.

❋❋❋❋❋

All this human and natural interaction is part of a larger tide that sweeps the seas of time. Early in the summer of the wedding, I started to dig a hole near a seasonally wet area on the northwest side of the land. Immediately I came up against a thick net of tangled roots, held together in a layer of crumbly, dry soil. It took an hour's work with an ax and a mattock to break through the roots to a fine grainy soil. I widened the hole, and commenced downward toward China.

This was also hard going. I encountered a thick, claylike soil that very soon in my excavation became moist. More digging, more widening of the hole, and then, quite suddenly, the gray, yellowish clay soil turned jet black and became decidedly wetter. I finally gave up and sat down to study the profile of the soil.

It consisted of a layer of duff or topsoil laid down year after year once the land was originally cleared about 350 years ago. Then there appeared the yellow clay and then dark wet clay. Given this thick foundation of impermeable clay, I could understand why in spring this section of the garden is under a foot or two of water in places, and to this day remains uncultivated.

A few weeks after I dug that hole, I noticed another example of the foundation of my garden and its surrounds. In preparation for yet another cluster of new houses in this formerly wooded area, a half a mile down the road, a huge cut had been gouged out of one of the hills. One day when no one was around I snuck onto the site to investigate and noticed that the subsoil consisted—literally—of sand dunes.

This section of land is thirty-five miles from the sea, and yet the sand at the construction site was as fine and light-colored as the sands of the best beaches in the region.

I knew just where the sands had come from.

Ten thousand years ago, just west of my garden, there was a lake. Over time the lake dried, and the strong northwestern winds, blowing across the dried lake bed, picked up the lighter sands and deposited them on the east side of the lake bed. Over the next three or four thousand years or so, a forest grew on top of those dunes.

❋❋❋❋❋

All gardens begin with groundwork, and all the grounds of the world are part of a larger ecological environment, or biome, from which they are forged. It was no different in the case of my grounds and my garden. The entire landscape in these parts is the handiwork of the ice.

Sixty thousand years ago in the northern hemisphere, the winters lengthened and the earth began to cool significantly so that snows began to build higher and higher each winter. Eventually, as a result of the cooling climate, the summers were not hot enough to melt the layers of winter snow. More snow accumulated year by year and decade by decade, until finally the accumulated snows of the North were so pressed down and lay so deep upon the solid earth beneath that they formed a base of ice that began to expand southward. As these great walls of ice moved, they crushed the earth in their path, picked up seemingly immovable heavy boulders, rode over the very mountaintops, scoured out river valleys, and pressed on inexorably—a dreadful, deathly wall of ice, cut through with deep valleys at the fringes, but still moving ever southward and carrying with it its massive payload of scraped earth and gravel and boulders.

And then, about twenty thousand years ago, the summers became warmer and managed, slowly, to melt away sections of the glacier. Decade after decade, generation after generation, for thousands of years, the ice melted. In Northeastern North America, where the glacier halted and drew back, it left behind its payload of sand and gravel in long terminal moraines. It deposited immense blocks of ice that melted down to form pools that are still with us today in the form of kettle-hole ponds. Within the icy body, serpentine rivers carrying loads of gravel slowed and melted and left behind long winding ridges known as eskers. And in some sections, deep holes developed in the ice, and within these holes were swirling waters, also carrying sand and gravel and small boulders, and these too settled to form small pyramid-like hills known as kames.

The glacier also left behind a scattering of whale-backed hills known as drumlins. The material inside these hills has layers of a mix of sand, gravel, and rocks known as glacial till, sometimes laid down in a uniform deposition, sometimes all mixed up together. Drumlins may also contain layers of clay, which it appears is the case with the Scratch Flat drumlin where my garden is located.

Generally speaking, drumlins are not ideal spots for gardens. In my garden, the soil consists of a mix of gravelly rocks and debris, stratified beds of clay soil that do not drain well in early spring, and wide areas that do drain, and none of these sections particularly fertile. It took years of manure and compost and seasons of plantings of winter rye and buckwheat and more manure and compost to coax even the seemingly slow growth that this garden demonstrates—as opposed to other gardens I know.

I didn't know any of this when I first moved onto the land, and in fact the soil in the gardens around my former house, at the lower end of the drumlin, was much better. I used to grow head-high beds of delphiniums there and was able to plant much earlier in the year than I can in the current garden.

One day, digging out a new flower bed in preparation for the wedding, I turned up the rib bone of a horse. It was about two feet long, yellowed with age, pocked and scribed and much gnawed by mice, and weathered by the acid soils and long winters. Hefting it absent-mindedly there in the spring sunshine, it suddenly struck me that I knew of this horse.

Shortly after I moved to my former house on the eastern slope of the drumlin, a large, red-haired man of about sixty showed up at the front door and asked if he could have a look around. He said he had grown up in the house as part of a large extended family. One night in the mid-1930s, when he was about eighteen, he and a cousin lowered themselves out of an upstairs bedroom window and hit the road. This was his first time back in forty-odd years.

We took a walk around the land while he reminisced about his childhood years on this small subsistence farm. The greatest shock to him was the white-pine woods. In his time, that section of the property had been an apple orchard. Among his many stories was one involving a half-wild white horse that no one could saddle. He and his friends used to jump on its back and go dashing bareback through the orchard while the horse would try to dislodge them by running under low-hanging branches. Later the horse went blind and spent its last years grazing under the apple trees, and when it finally died his family hauled it up to the back wall and buried it.

Over the next thirty years as, little by little, stone by stone, I have slowly cleared the land to make room for new gardens, I have turned up other evidence of the various families that lived on this land since 1810, when the original house on the property was built: Shoe leather, old tools, a bridle, medicine bottles, ink bottles, buttons, shards of willowware, shards of Canton china, bits of glass, bits of stoneware, pottery, clay marbles, a doll's head, knives and forks, and leaky tin pots. Also arrowheads. This was the Nashoba Valley, one of the oldest extant farming regions in the Northeast, having been worked by the English since 1654, and for nearly three thousand years before that by the Native Americans. In fact, Christianized Indians planted the first apple trees in the valley—Roxbury russets—brought over by John Winthrop in 1630.

The first arrowhead I found was a nondescript, modest point

from what is known as the Late Woodland culture, a very recent group as far as Native American history is concerned. The new farmers, which is to say the English, German, Italians, and Greeks who worked this land over the 352-year period of European cultivation, would turn up arrowheads during spring plowing. Some of these were saved by the local historical society, and with a little care you can work backwards through the buried layers of Native American history, ending with a singular point that now resides in the collection, a so-called Paleo point, which is about five inches long and has a fluted groove down the center.

In the time of the Paleo people, some ten thousand years ago, the garden patch where I found the horse bone was a dry heath-covered hill on the eastern side of the dried-up lake bed. Moving across the landscape were herds of mastodons, giant elk, barren-ground caribou, and other species of Pleistocene megafauna, all of which the Indians hunted.

Slowly, over the millennia, as the climate warmed, the human uses of the land changed. Hunting as a sole means of subsistence declined and was augmented by plant gathering. Then, about three thousand years ago, formerly hunter-gathering cultures developed agriculture. With the arrival of the English, farming became the main source of sustenance, and in time the main economy of the region. The valley was best known for apple growing, but by 1900 farmers were also producing dairy, hogs, and beef, some of which was exported to England.

Agriculture is now in decline around here. Most of the old orchards are gone, except for one publicly owned tract that was saved by the town in remembrance. The farmers who still work these lands might as well work for nonprofit agencies, such is their income, and slowly, farm by farm, field by field, and lot by lot, new houses and small electronic-based industries have moved in.

The death knell of the agricultural economy of the town began to toll around the early 1960s, when the state laid out a major highway through the western part of the town. For a while, after I first moved in, the essence of the old farming community endured. There were five working farms on Scratch Flat, with hayfields just across the road from my first garden that dropped down to the floodplain of the north-running stream in a series of terraced steps. I could look out over the fields in those days and see a veritable pastoral, a tumbled-down barn, with cows grazing in the background. The road that separated the house from the fields was so quiet and untrafficked you could lie down in the middle of the street on a Sunday morning and watch the barn swallows coursing over the fields.

The town itself was almost Dickensian in its eccentricities. There was a movie theater in the center of town set at the edge of a cornfield. You could smell the ripe corn on hot summer nights whenever you stepped out of the theater. Two old brothers maintained a hardware store in the center of the town, and when one of them died, the other closed the shop and never touched another item. If you looked in through the darkened windows, in the middle of the sales floor you could see a perfectly maintained Pen Yann motorboat from the 1930s.

There was a strange, very narrow barnlike building just west of the town center where a stone-deaf Polish man had a sharpening shop that no one ever seemed to visit—except me. I used to get my scythe blades sharpened there, indicating through sign what I wanted. His deafness probably didn't matter. I'm not sure he spoke English.

Closer at hand, in the town center, was a small general store, also rarely visited, and run by a very formal older man named Mr. Smith, who dressed always in a hound's-tooth jacket, an ironed white shirt, and conservative tie. He was a taciturn old gentleman with steel-rimmed glasses and watery blue eyes and he stood alone behind his counter every day, including Christmas and Thanksgiving.

About ten years after the highway blasted through the town, the inevitable came to pass. A computer company constructed a monstrous temple to industry behind the barn of the scythe sharpener. The company bought the barn and tore it down; along with the better part of the pear orchard that had grown on a hillside at the edge of town. The hardware store closed after the last brother died, and the shop reopened, selling auto parts. Old Mr. Smith died, and his general store became a lawyer's office. New faces appeared in the town. The movie theater was torn down and replaced by a chain hardware store. The hardware store was torn down and replaced by an immense, overwhelmingly out-of-scale Toyota car lot that virtually everyone in the town hated. Its glistening vehicles were laid out in shining rows over the southwestern slopes of the cornfields that used to scent the town on summer evenings.

A few of the farms held on in spite of these changes. And in fact, driving into the community from the east or west, one might be struck by the fact that the main road is still lined with fields and farm stands, as opposed to the fast-food joints of nearby towns.

But all that may be doomed. The current surge in local farming notwithstanding, the town fathers appear to have their eyes on a different sort of future, and it does not include agriculture.

As the generally rural character of the town slipped toward suburbanity, as traffic increased, and housing and commercial development grew ever closer to the fields of Scratch Flat, I found myself taking my garden project more seriously, planting more, digging out new beds, planting more flowering trees, digging more frog ponds, and designing new hedge allées. The place became a sanctuary for me in the traditional sense, and also a metaphor. By creating this garden in the face of the deluge, I felt I was making a statement of how I believed the world should be.

There was nothing new in this. All the gardens of the West, starting with the watered gardens of Uruk and the hanging gardens of Babylon, through to the orderly landscapes of the Renaissance gardens of Italy and France, served as hedges—literally—against the noisy, chaotic squalor and dangers of the urban streets and the bandit-ridden violence of the countryside.

Here on Scratch Flat this chaos of the real world becomes all the more clear to me whenever I sally forth from my sanctuary on some errand after a long spell of working in the garden. The real world comes crashing in: immense SUVs appear in the rearview mirror, bearing down on me and hot to get somewhere, and everyone rushing and wheeling along at high and dangerous rates of speed, when in fact they are probably going nowhere except to the post office. My whole perception of time has to shift, and it takes me a while to snap out of my reveries and catch up with the world.

The great consolation is that I know I will return. The trees will not have changed position; the bees and the ants will still be foraging in the flowers. And in spite of all this rushing around and getting and spending, the current world will eventually accumulate in the soils beneath just as it always has—car parts, farm equipment, bottles and buttons, china plates, horse bones, arrowheads and spear points. Nevertheless, for now, in my time, the garden stands as bulwark against modernity.

2.

The Mead

a dandelion
now and then interrupting
the butterfly's dream

✳ CHIYO-NI

In 1503, the German engraver and artist Albrecht Dürer painted a watercolor called *The Great Piece of Turf*, which depicts in detail virtually all the plants growing in a small section of earth. This watercolor is much admired by art critics for its rendering of the visual and poetic beauty contained in wild nature and for its botanical accuracy. The painting was created outside Vienna—in spring, judging from the plants in flower—but what is interesting from an American point of view is that many of the flowers and grasses shown in the watercolor can be found here in the New World. If you look around, you could find the same plants in your own backyard if you have deigned to allow a few weeds to take hold.

Between the maze and lawn there is a patch of turf that I have intentionally allowed to go wild. The plot itself, which in some ways is the most interesting section of the garden, is only seventeen feet by eight. On the west side there is a hedge of Sargent crab apples. There are rose of Sharon trees on the south side, a privet hedge to the east, and on the north, toward the house, a wall of rhododendrons, hollies, and hydrangeas. All of these were planted years ago as part of my evolving grand plan for the grounds, but the plants in the patch of earth inside this small garden room came along on their own, and the place has become, quite by accident, one of my favorite parts of the property. Without any effort, a florid mix of three or four species of grass has taken hold there, mixed in with cinquefoil, escaped sedums, ajuga, gill-over-the-ground, and speedwell, all tangled in with Siberian iris, daylilies, and bee balm and other mints. Beyond these, dandelions, daisies, Queen Anne's lace, plantains, dock, hawkweed, yarrow, and bindweed—to name but a few—fill in the void, running and rambling every which way and creating, in this tiny space, a dense thicket of vegetation so rank and so tangled you cannot take a single step without crushing some innocent flowering plant or routing some insect, or even a frog or a snake.

By midsummer I always see here the suspended and darting forms of hoverflies, whose great claim to fame is that they can fly *backwards*. Unlike other insects, which usually have four wings, flies only have two. But they do have rudimentary wings that act as stabilizers which help certain species of flies maneuver quickly so that they can hover in midair, dash forward, turn in place, and also fly backwards.

The hoverflies always appear on June 10th, or at least I always first notice them on that date. They dart here and there over the weedy jungle, or hang above the grass like helicopters, and then dash forward, only to return to their original space. I have noticed that two or sometimes three of them will hang close together, and then dash at one another in a frenzy, spreading mayhem among the other hoverflies in the area. Although this hang-and-dash flight is part of their feeding method—they are predatory, beneficial insects for gardeners—I suspect that there may be some territorial intent in the attacks and counterattacks on one another.

Also passing through this greeny tangle are dragonflies, such as the little red meadowhawks and the big green darners, which sweep over the patch on hot days and cast about over the mead that serves as a lawn just beyond the shrub wall. A wide array of butterflies, including red admirals, tiger swallowtails, painted ladies, and viceroys, also occurs here, along with the related skippers and moths. Then, in late summer, the gems of the garden move in.

Every morning in late August, draping the seed heads and the last of the daisy fleabanes and the goldenrods and asters, are necklaces of dew-spangled webs created by the large black-and-yellow orb weaver spiders. As nature photographers know, mornings, when the dew is on the vine, is the best time to spot these jeweled necklaces. Often the proprietor is not in sight. She (the female is the weaver) waits in the wings, connected to her web by a trapline that vibrates whenever an insect becomes ensnared.

The females are the larger of the sexes; the males are smaller, more obscure, and lead a dangerous life. After mating, the female may consume him if he's not fast enough to make his break, which, as it turns out, some manage to do. A recent study of the genus indicates that a few males are able to survive their first tryst and live on to impregnate other females. They also seem to seek out the younger, virgin spiders.

Also evident in this grassroot jungle are the night-hunting wolf spiders. These range around the garden after dark, running down their prey like wolves or pouncing on them like foxes. They're brown and gray and relatively obscure but very common, with many different species in North America and worldwide. I see them often in other parts of the garden, sometimes carrying their young on their backs.

Along with firefly hunts, one of the most popular night expeditions with the various children of the Vicarage Garden is to range through the garden rooms at night hunting "wolves." We all take flashlights out and search the grassroots until we see tiny red garnets gleaming in the vegetation—the red eyes of the wolf spiders.

This great tangle of vegetation lies south of the boundary of mostly evergreen shrubs with two sets of columnar arborvitae guarding two garden gates, leading to the southernmost garden rooms. In front of this wall is a boundary of flower beds, and in front of that is a semicircular lawn, a *tapis vert* in Edith Wharton's ever-Continental parlance.

The shorn lawn, the invention of eighteenth-century English estate grounds, is now the pride and joy and most blatant statement of the typical American suburban landscape. A vast amount of arable land in the United States is covered by lawn, about 30 million acres all told, which is about three times the amount of land devoted to that other monocultural grass, corn. Most of these lawns are relatively small, but if turned over for vegetable gardens, any one of them could supply a small family with a substantial amount of fresh produce in season.

Nevertheless, in spite of their tedious uniformity, contrary to my tastes in garden design, I have one. Sort of. I rarely tend the plot, and I mow (as little as possible) with a hand-propelled reel mower, in contrast to the huge riding mowers favored by my neighbors in a relatively new development up the road, known (with not so much as a hint of irony) as the Quail Hollow Estates. Never mind that quail do not occur in this region and that the "estates" are crowded together cheek by jowl with no gardens to speak of.

Save for one organically maintained, florid property that stands out in contrast to the other houses, this development is basically a dead zone, a colony of mausoleums. You rarely see people there; the windows and doors are closed to maintain an artificial, climate-controlled interior atmosphere, and the grounds are virtually toxic. You can smell pesticides and herbicides when you walk through the development on certain days, as well as the sour odor of artificially dyed wood chips that are spread anywhere on the properties where a weed might dare to appear. I would not want any of my children to play in the yards there for fear of poisoning.

My own lawn is more of a meadow or flowering mead than a formal, shorn greensward. It consists of a mix of native and non-native grasses, and when it is newly cut does have the appearance of a green carpet. But also growing here are the dreaded weeds so despised by my neighbors. I have allowed chickweeds, violets, dandelions, speedwell, cinquefoil, buttercups, and other volunteers to join the company of grasses and clovers that I have planted. In some cases, in order to counter the dead spaces left by crabgrasses, I have even planted undesirables, such as ajuga or creeping thyme and gill-over-the-ground. All this is maintained without benefit of fertilizers or herbicides.

This practice has created a changing palette of colors throughout the growing season. In spring, it is characterized by splashes of blues and purples and white from the violets, ajugas, and quaker-ladies, with dashes of yellow from the dandelions and butter-cups. In late summer, sections of the "lawn" turn purple from the creeping thyme, with another burst of yellow from the sedums, and in November the grasses assume the deep green shades of a Renaissance painting. The mead—which serves as the footpad of the goose in my *patte d'oie* design—is about twenty-four hundred square feet, a mere thirty paces or so in any direction, and yet I have counted here four or five species of grasses, along with the company of weeds, some of which, such as mustard, docks, and plantain, I do cut down. I'm sure I am missing some species in my various surveys, but all told there are at least four or five times the number of flowering plants in this single area than there were in the former pine woods, and far more than grow in the monocul-tural lawns of the Quail Hollow Estates.

This type of lawn management has also encouraged, along with a welcome diversity of plants, a bounty of small spiders and insects, such as ants. Most of these soil-dwelling ant species con-struct underground nests. You can often find the little piles of their excavations in among the grasses. Below ground, the colony is ruled and produced by a queen mother, a larger version of the workers, with a longer abdomen, who may live on for a number of years. She is tended by a few ineffectual male dandies who die not long after mating, and also a colony of workers who range out from the nest each day to forage on seeds and, among some spe-cies, other insects.

Some of these local ants work as herders, a habit that has fostered another favorite adventure for the various generations of children around this compound. On warm days, if you search carefully through the flowers of the garden beds, especially along the stems and on the undersides of leaves, you can find ant shepherds tending small flocks of sheep-like, grazing aphids. In fact, the ants are not exactly herding, they are merely feeding on the sweet honeydew that is excreted by the aphids, but in the process, they will protect their flocks from local predators.

Because of this habit of feeding on honeydew, certain species of ants, such as the cornfield ant, will give off a lemony odor when crushed. I have used this characteristic to amuse and horrify visiting children by allowing ants to crawl over my wrist and then consuming them with relish, like an anteater. They have the slight acid flavor of lemons, with a hint of verbena, and as long as you bite quickly enough, they will not get the chance to bite you back. I learned this trick years ago when I was working at a nature center and guiding schoolchildren through the woods. If ever I lost their attention, I would turn over a log, catch a few ants, and eat them—much to the children's horror and delight.

For a few years, as I cleared off the land to make new garden beds, I would come across large, mounded piles of fluffy soil—the nests of the Allegheny mound ant, a species that ranges all along the eastern coast of North America. For a while I used to tolerate these seemingly inoffensive, interesting additions to the garden, until I tripped one day and landed with my wrist in a mound and was instantly attacked and bitten. I later learned that these mound builders can actually clear the herbaceous plants around their mounds by injecting formic acid into the stems. After that, whenever I found them, I uprooted the mounds and evicted them.

There was one other pest species I was forced to deal with to protect my so-called lawn, and this was the grub of the Japanese beetle, an invader whose populations seem to periodically wax and wane. I refused to employ pesticides to control these devils and took to digging them out patch by patch. Fortunately, I had a great ally in this endeavor — my wife's dog, the Jack Russell terrier, who adopted me as his boon hunting companion in his otherwise circumscribed life as soon as he moved onto the property. He used to track me everywhere I went. If I went for a walk to the hemlock grove behind the house, he would join me, sometimes tagging at my heels, sometimes ranging out ahead of me in ever widening gyres, and poking his black nose into every hole, hollow, rock crevice, tree crevice, leaf pile, brush pile, puddle, and pit he could find. In the garden, he was also there. If I was in the process of digging a hole to plant a new tree, he would stand beside me, ever alert, his head cocked, watching my work intently. If I deserted this task and moved over to clip a hedge, he would trot behind at my heels. Waiting. And if ever I was on my knees with my hands deep in the good earth — about at his level, in other words — I would hear his snuffling and glance over. There he'd be, cheek to jowl with me, eyes fixed on the ground, ears perked forward, ready for action.

In time, I taught him to help me dig out weeds, and even trained him to dig holes for tulip planting. I had but to pat the earth and command him to attack, and he would dig furiously until I called him off, thereby excavating a perfect tulip-sized hole.

This habit, I learned, also proved useful for grub hunting. After turning over a divot to expose the inevitable grub — or grubs — I would simply squish them, replace the divot, and move on. Of course, the dog was there at my ankles, and one day on a lark I commanded him to "*Eat!*" He dove right in, gobbled up the grub, and began to dig for more. From then on, I simply had to move around the lawn turning up turf so he could feed on the grubs. Within a season, in this manner, with his help, I managed to eliminate all the grubs from the lawn.

The back lawn is not the only area in the garden devoted to grass, however. All the various rooms, flower beds, and vegetable plots are interconnected with grassy paths, which I mow periodically. Here, in these sometimes weedy interstices, I find other species of insects such as spittlebugs, leafhoppers, and a wide variety of beetles, including the beautiful jade-green tiger beetles. These latter are speedy little predators on garden pests, which run down their prey in the same style as the wolf spiders. It is a large order of beetle, with more than two thousand species all told.

When I first started with this property I was less inclined to have a lawn at all. I originally maintained a cleared wildflower meadow that I mowed with a scythe. The main stretch of this particular habitat was the swath of cleared land that led from the house down to the road. I allowed the plants here to grow knee-high, and then, after the first flowering of the weeds, set out to mow.

I very much enjoyed this work, especially on warm summer mornings when the air was alive with birdsong. But it had its drawbacks. The grounds never did have the semi-shorn look that I wanted to achieve—probably because I never fully developed the fine art of scything. There were always messy, humped tangles of grasses that the scythe blade missed. But there was a larger problem.

Scything is beautiful, silent, smooth work. You move down one row, turn, and come back up the other way, laying down the blades in rows, with the scent of fresh-cut grass filling the air, along with the sounds of birds and the swish of the blade. With each sweep of the scythe on these summer mornings, I would set in flight a host of crickets, Carolina grasshoppers, leafhoppers, and other grass-dwelling species of insects. But because of the silence, and the slow approach, and probably the length of the blade, I would periodically kill outright some innocent snake or toad or frog.

Partly for this reason, I eventually gave up the practice, except for the little interconnecting paths and the orchard and the rooms of weeds, grasses, mosses, and ajuga behind the hornbeam wall on the south side of the property.

For a while to keep the lawn cut I used a power mower, which effectively evicted all the grass-dwelling denizens and which I came to detest because of the noise and stink and the maintenance (not to mention the environmental consequences—power mowers are major sources of air pollution and noise). After that I used an old hand mower to maintain the grass sward of the *patte d'oie*. Unfortunately the reel mower, even at its highest setting, keeps the grass too short to attract in any number the leafhoppers and spittlebugs, toads, and snakes, and I sometimes wonder if my little world here would be better off if I simply went back to mowing the property with a scythe and risked losing a few frogs and snakes each season. However, I learned that, in spite of the prevalence of riding mowers for even the smallest suburban lawn, companies are now manufacturing lighter reel mowers and these can be adjusted to higher levels than the old-fashioned types. I went out and bought one, thus saving a nation of small creatures that live in grassy habitats.

✳✳✳✳✳

So much of the lawn care in this fast-developing region where the garden is located is devoted to killing indiscriminately everything but grass. But there is another disadvantage to a greensward, even an organically maintained, shorn lawn, that is often overlooked, and that is the effect this vast monocultural landscape has on wood frogs.

Almost any area where there are woods, except perhaps for upland ridges, will have a few low spots that hold water throughout the spring and into the early summer. These temporary ponds, or vernal pools, are veritable cradles of life, the mating and birthing places for any number of amphibians, insects, and crustaceans. One of the most obvious of these is the wood frog.

In late February or early March, as soon as the snow is off the ground in northern areas, if you are anywhere near a damp woodland you may hear the quacking calls of a small flock of invisible ducks. Approach the sound of the calls and the ducks will disappear.

The quacking is not caused by some as-yet-undiscovered species of invisible duck, it is in fact the call of breeding wood frogs, and as soon as they sense the approach of danger they will fall silent.

The adults are about two and a half inches in length, and can be easily recognized by their black masks—they look a little like amphibious raccoons. In later winter the males migrate to the ponds and begin calling, either to attract mates or to warn away other males. Once they have mated, the female lays some three thousand eggs, suspended in two firm jelly coats and clumped together. The eggs will hatch quickly—in four or five days, generally—and develop into tadpoles that also quickly turn into froglets. They soon disperse into the surrounding forest before the pond waters dry up, usually around May or June in the vernal pool just north of my garden. The frogs spend the rest of the warm season feeding on caterpillars, slugs, worms, beetles, and other invertebrates of the forest floor. They range widely, and the fact that I see them often from June through September in the garden speaks well, I think, of my messy garden practices.

Wood frogs despise open, cleanly cut, sunny lawns or golf courses, not to mention things such as parking lots and driveways. The research that uncovered this disturbing fact came to pass as a result of a carefully monitored vernal pool that was threatened by the expansion of a parking lot for a shopping mall that was under construction in a town about twenty miles south of my home territory. For once, the developers willingly followed the letter of local wetland-protection laws. The builders preserved the vernal pool and left a wide strip of native vegetation around the little pond. The herpetologist overseeing this conservation effort continued to follow the wood frog population in the pond after the work was done. But in spite of the fact that every precaution was taken in order to protect as much local habitat as possible, the population in the vernal pool began to decline.

The herpetologist continued to track the resident frogs, and came to realize that they were avoiding the surrounding parking lots. Further research indicated that they also refused to cross open lawns, preferring wherever they could find it the weedy strips and brushy edges of suburban yards, which in any self-respecting, clean suburb are few. The result is that in suburban areas, the once-common wood frog is beginning to decline.

※※※※※

Conservation of wood frogs is perhaps not the primary concern of the home owners in developments such as the Quail Hollow Estates, nor is the cultivation, much less the encouragement, of weeds, like white clover—which I have actually planted on my lawn. Here also in my yard are all the usual low-growing weeds and escaped groundcovers that make up the tapestry of the mead. And at the brushy edges of the shrub walls I also encourage the taller weeds, such as yarrow and Queen Anne's lace, daisies, New England aster, dame's rocket, and bouncing Bet.

I did not plant any of these handsome flowers; they simply arrived on their own to gladden the garden. Birds, winds, jettisoned potting soil from plant purchases, and no doubt a few plants that had lain dormant as seeds in the former forest soil ever since this land was seriously cultivated by the first settlers on these grounds, eventually brought these plants to fruition. Weed seeds can sleep for generations and then burst into flower once they get to the surface and the sun.

Some of the escapees have created fortuitous beds. After I planted the maze, for example, I had to mow the grasses that grew on the courses, or paths, between the hedges. This was not easy going, and had to be accomplished with a power mower and involved a great deal of backing and filling in order to get around the twelve bends in the maze. As the hedges grew higher they shaded the paths, and periwinkles got in. Within a few years they spread throughout the maze floor, creating a fine evergreen bed with a narrow footpath winding through.

Other weeds I do have to do battle with, else they take over the whole garden. Garlic mustard is one of these. I've been vigilant about this plant and so far have kept it away. The tiny white chickweeds that jump up in any cultivated open soil in spring I also have to hoe down each year, and I have to keep a vigil lest black swallowwort invades, or even worse, mile-a-minute vine, which has been moving into the region.

The worst of the invaders on these grounds, however, are the woody shrubs—winged euonymus, autumn olive, multiflora rose, and the highly aggressive oriental bittersweet that climbs over every trunk, trellis, shrub, or hedge if it gets a chance.

Other flowers and shrubs I have imported, or stolen, from other properties. I am by nature a notorious trespasser and as such favor explorations of abandoned houses and the ruins of forgotten and overlooked gardens. Here I have found, along with the usual assortment of popular flowers such as daylilies, old-fashioned ornamental plants now out of vogue, such as valerian, sweet William, bluebells, and Saint John's wort.

For several years running I used to raid an old ruined farmhouse for its struggling copper beech sprouts. These I would bring home and nurse along for a few years, only to watch them succumb. But there have also been success stories. Not a hundred yards from my own property, in nearby woods, I found a poor, light-starved rowan tree, which I dug up and brought and planted in the sun. It has thrived happily. The same thing happened with a scraggly sheep laurel I found under nearby power lines. In that same part of Scratch Flat, down in a wet valley of undetermined ownership, I found a sad little rhodora, the subject of Emerson's poem of the same name and the source of the famous line "beauty is its own excuse for being."

I dug it up and replanted it in the garden, and now, in contrast to Emerson's secretive rhodora, which hid away unseen beside a shaded pool, it holds an admirable spot just outside the dining room window.

In the early years of the garden I became a manner of hunter-gatherer of plants, I caught a strange variety of privet that had gone wild in a property scheduled to be developed. At another site of a teardown (of which there are many in this region of increasing wealth), I stole antique roses of obscure identity. I have also managed to acquire old delphiniums, lamiums, feverfew, Jacob's ladder, and one of my finest trophies, a planting of peonies, all sad and thin and rarely flowering, as far as I could tell. I brought them home and put them in a bed of their own. The following spring they flourished, and have continued to flower profusely.

For years I felt the need to have a mulberry tree in the garden, a plant used by my hero in these matters, Andrew Jackson Downing. I searched through local nurseries and catalogues, but all I could find were new varieties of camperdown mulberries, twisted, sickly-looking trees. Nevertheless, I persisted and began hunting old properties in the region, still without luck. Then one day, in a tangle of multiflora rose and black birch, in a wild section of the compound, I found one. It was a slender, struggling thing, half-buried by invasive plants, but I charged in with a machete and a mattock, cut everything away from the trunk of the mulberry, dug it up, and transplanted it to a section of the garden where I maintained other rescued trees, including the rowan tree and a basswood I had saved.

Still more flowers came from my neighbor, Rick Findlay, the son of an azalea collector from Westport, Massachusetts. Mr. Findlay has followed in his father's footsteps and become an eclectic collector himself. His property was one of the earliest farms in the town and already had a diverse planting of trees and shrubs. But after he moved in, he began to bring in more. There was already a collection of daylilies on the property, but he started amassing wallflowers in his various garden patches, followed by more daylilies, then varieties of shrubs and trees, more perennial beds, ground covers, and finally, a large collection of rhododendrons. In the end, he estimates that he has about a thousand varieties of trees, shrubs, and herbaceous plants on his grounds, if you count the number of cultivars. He often thins his collections, and over the years has supplied me with wild gingers, lamiums, wallflowers, dianthus, azaleas, daylilies, as well as numerous redbuds, viburnums, and one or two Carolina snowbells and a Carolina silverbell.

All these rescued trees and stolen flowers and shrubs and weeds offer a pleasing and perennial tapestry over the seasons of the year. But they have also offered a lot of good stories for the children of the garden: Bouncing Bet, for example, is supposedly named for an energetic washerwoman. Black-eyed Susan spent her days looking for her companion, sweet William. Saint John's wort holds devils at bay. Leopard's bane and wolf's bane and bugbane keep the leopards and wolves and insect pests out of the garden; dogbane wards off stray dogs, and forget-me-not, along with its memory encouragement, marks the entrance to a fairy cave.

I have taken advantage of this flower folklore to weave elaborate stories of the night adventures of the unseen fairy kingdom that is known to exist side by side with the everyday world here on Scratch Flat. It is a well-known fact, for example, that the fairy ring mushrooms grow in a circle, indicating the spot where a fairy dance was held the night before. Puck hides in a cowslip; Titania sleeps on a bed of thyme, canopied with woodbine, musk rose, and eglantine, and all manner of fairies, gnomes, elves, and sprites come out on moonlit nights to cavort in garden grounds.

These tales have not gone unnoticed by the various generations of children. Five-year-olds, who are known to have better eyesight than adults, have described normally invisible events to me. One of the children saw an actual fairy procession one morning. They came out from under a planting of delphiniums and marched around the bed and disappeared. They were dressed, I was told, in blue-and-white-striped trousers, with green waistcoats and red vests, striped sashes, and colorful floppy hats beset with bird feathers. The lady fairies wore silken flowing skirts, had circlets of flowers woven in their hair, and were playing tambourines and tiny cymbals.

Such is the value of a great patch of turf. Fairies, like wood frogs, do not favor manicured lawns.

3.

The Wildwood

First he ate some lettuces and some French beans; and then he ate some radishes; and then, feeling rather sick, he went to look for some parsley.

❋ Beatrix Potter,
The Tale of Peter Rabbit

Sometimes I thread my way through the woods on the west side of the garden wall and stand at the edge of one of the last farm fields in this region, looking over the patchwork of the cultivated lands of Scratch Flat. I used to know people in this area who claimed to be descendants of the Paleo-Indians who first hunted this region, after the ice sheets drew back. One of them claimed that by means of ritual chanting and drumming, through a process known to anthropologists as ceremonial time, you could obliterate linear time and be in places as they were long ago, as many as fifteen thousand years ago, for example.

Were I standing in this spot at some point between the retreat of the ice and the extinction of the great mammals of the Pleistocene era, I might have seen, grazing on the flatlands below me, herds of mastodons and barren-ground caribou. In fact, at the very spot where I was standing, a now-extinct short-nosed bear or a pack of dire wolves may have lingered, eyeing the herds. For that matter, there might have been, at some point in the two- or three-thousand-year reign of their culture, a band of fur-clad mammoth hunters crouched here—also watching the herds below.

All this is real. And as my friend, the descendant of these Paleo people, has explained to me repeatedly, all that separates *us* from *them*, is time, and time, as theoretical physics tells us, is not as orderly and fixed as we generally assume it to be. The past isn't dead; it isn't even past, as William Faulkner pointed out.

The fact is, any backyard in the whole northern tier of the North American continent probably had mastodons standing around in gardens where the tea roses now bloom, or giant sloths in the vegetable patches, and packs of dire wolves bedded down where a flowering crab now blooms.

As was her custom, the English Lady summed up the situation when I tried to describe all this to her: "Do you mean to tell me," she asked, raising her left eyebrow, "there were pachyderms in the pachysandras?"

My attention to the details of the natural history of a garden is hardly a new exercise. In the late eighteenth century, the English curate Gilbert White made a deep study of the plants and animals of his gardens and the surrounding region of Selborne, in Hampshire. He worked by direct observation of birds and mammals, and the habits of insects and the seasons of the flowering plants in the area. The world was new to science in his time; there was much that was not actually known, and there were many misconceptions. The migration of birds, among other things, was not thoroughly understood. It was believed, for example, that swifts hibernated in winter.

In 1789, White published a compilation of a series of letters describing his local world called *The Natural History and Antiquities of Selborne*, a book that has been in print ever since it was published, and one of the first detailed descriptions of the behavior and life ways of certain species of animals, birds in particular.

Roughly fifty years later, the American naturalist Henry Thoreau maintained an extensive fourteen-volume journal of observations along the same lines, focusing on Concord, Massachusetts, and its environs. Thoreau's journals are considered to be his greatest work. They are daily accounts of his rambles around Walden and Concord documenting, among many other natural events, the flowering dates of plants, the water depth of Walden and its sister, White Pond, the arrival and departure of pond ice and snow, the records of migratory-bird arrivals and departures, and a myriad of similar small, generally unnoticed events that wheel through the four seasons.

As the climate has slowly changed, these records have provided a useful baseline for biologists tracking the advance of the warming trends that are occurring worldwide. The same has proved true with White's records, as well as the notes of generations of English gardeners. As Mrs. Theodosia Huntingfield has pointed out, the English cottage gardeners were assiduous journal keepers.

Thoreau and White both worked from firsthand observation of the natural world, and both recorded local nature lore among the country people. White in particular was interested in this subject, as the full title of his book suggests. The contribution to natural science of these two has been invaluable. But folklore itself can sometimes substantiate the changes in the natural world that take place over time. The local Native Americans around Scratch Flat had folktales concerning a being known as the Yaquaway, which had long red hair and huge curving teeth—clearly a woolly mammoth or a mastodon. There is also a folkloric record of a great flood, inspired no doubt by actual floods caused by the rising waters as the glaciers melted, which created huge inland lakes and inland seas and raised mighty rushing rivers everywhere.

In our time, prime among this vast company of English cottage garden watchers, as well as the self-taught local naturalists such as Henry Thoreau and Gilbert White, is an Oxford-educated ecologist named Jennifer Owen who, starting in 1956, conducted a scientific survey of the plants and animals of her tiny garden in Leicester, in the heart of the English Midlands. As with Gilbert White, she carried on her study for the next three and a half decades, documenting in detail the myriad life forms that appeared in her ever-so-ordinary cottage garden. Some of these animals, such as the insects and small mammals and nesting birds, were year-round residents. Some passed through from time to time, or spent a few years nesting or breeding and then disappeared. But by the time she stopped counting, in 2001, she had amassed a record of forty-four species of birds, seven species of mammals, nearly two thousand different insects, as well as more than a hundred species of spiders and woodlice, and over four hundred species of plants. All told the number of different plants and animals living among her ordinary cottage garden of food crops and flowers amounted to 2,673. She calculated that if she had kept counting she could have found many more, but by age seventy-five she was confined to a wheelchair and had to cut short her field studies.

Although she maintained a garden containing many native

species of local flowers, her garden was not limited to plants of the British Isles. As with most gardeners, she grew the usual number of nonnative plants. In fact, of the four hundred plants she had in her garden, the majority were cultivated; the others came in on their own in the form of what many, I suppose, would term "weeds."

❋ ❋ ❋ ❋ ❋

Among the associated company of the children of the garden, there was one of the second generation who, for a while, assumed an inordinate interest in woolly mammoths. This came to pass partly because of my bedtime stories of the mastodons, mammoths, dire wolves, and caribou who once lived on Scratch Flat, and partly because, to encourage at least one paleontologist or archaeologist in the family, I plied him with books on mammoths. By fifth grade he had become an authority on the subject.

Things have become decidedly tamer in the forest beyond the western wall. Nonetheless, denizens of this wilder tract have periodically wandered through the garden, thanks in part to this extensive woods, which, if you count the farms and wooded corridors between developments, extends all the way up to Canada. Moose and bears are periodically seen around the nearby fields. One night, a bear wandered into my garden and bent in half a steel post for a bird feeder in order to help itself to the seed; another bear climbed onto the porch of my next-door neighbor's to help itself to birdseed. Bobcats cross the yard; I see their tracks in the fresh snow on winter mornings. And in the most exciting spotting of all, one June morning a mountain lion sauntered by.

But along with visiting deer, foxes, bobcats, and coyotes, it is the smaller mammals such as skunks, possums, raccoons, woodchucks, and, of course, squirrels, chipmunks, and mice, that are the most common mammalian residents or visitors to the garden.

On the first day of winter one year, shortly after a light snowfall, I set out with my daughter, who was at the time the only girl in this troop of children, to see who in this wider family of mammals that live or pass through the garden had come calling in the night. It was a day not unlike any of the 364 other days that I walk the grounds, except that this was the official beginning of winter and the snow had created a blank slate whereon was written the stories of the night.

We began, as do so many garden expeditions, at the back door of the porch and set out past the terrace and the ground covers and the border of sentinel boxwoods, where we immediately discovered the tracks of some unidentified occupant of our own house. It was a small mammal who had emerged from beneath the glassed conservatory that serves as the dining room. It nosed around the bird feeder and then wandered aimlessly among the plantings of hollies, boxwoods, and the fishpond, and then set out in a winding path across the lawn.

The snow was fluffy in this area and the paw prints were indistinct, smaller than a possum's or a skunk's—the likely candidates—but too big for the other cohabitant of our house, the white-footed mouse. A chipmunk was also a possibility, but most of them were sound asleep in their burrows at that time of year. Chipmunks do not actually hibernate. They simply spend a lot of time sleeping in the bedrooms of their vast network of tunnels, which have hollowed-out chambers, some of which are reserved for sleeping quarters, some for bathrooms, and some for storage. They do wake up periodically, however, if the weather is warm enough, but this had been an early cold winter, with snow in November and a big storm in early December, so no sane chipmunk would be abroad in such conditions.

The other possibility was that the tracks were made by a rat. I have had rats at the bird feeder from time to time. In fact, although people may not realize it, almost any semi-urban suburb may have a visiting, or even resident, rat from time to time.

There are three species of rat in New England, the black rat, the Norway rat, and the wood rat. This latter is a now-rare native who generally prefers forested areas away from houses. It is distinguished from the other two by its furred tail, and the fact that, in contrast to its fellow rats, it is fair-minded. It likes to decorate its nest with shining objects such as coins or wedding rings, but will graciously leave a gift to replace the stolen item—a pebble, for example.

The black rat is more of a rogue. It favors seaport towns and docks, and is the rat that is responsible for the spread of the Black Death. The third of these rodents, the Norway rat, is the common city rat of sewers and streets, although it can also be found in the country, around barns and farmyards.

A few years before our winter tracking expedition, a Norway rat took up residence under the floor of our dining room. The other resident animal in our house at that time was the Jack Russell terrier, a breed known for its boundless energy, its singular perseverance in the face of a mission, and the fact that it despises rats. Perhaps needless to say, the presence of these two species in more or less the same quarters did not bode well for the rat.

Said rat arrived at our house in the dead of a cold winter and selected a crawl space beneath the dining room for its living quarters. We could see him from time to time, feeding like a chipmunk beneath the nearby bird feeder, and from the perspective of the breakfast table, he didn't look particularly evil or vicious. He had a healthy brown coat and appeared to be nothing more than a picturesque wild animal, and if it were not for the persistence of the dog, we might have let him stay.

But inasmuch as this particular dog was a Jack Russell, once he smelled the rat, he became obsessed. He lost interest in the primary pleasure of his small life—food—took up the cause, and moved into the dining room. He posted himself above the rat's resting places, whining and scratching the floor. He would leave from time to time, eat quickly, and then return to his work. We always knew exactly where the rat was under the floor, since the dog would move to different spots around the room, snuffling and scratching. He actually began to lose weight; such was his obsession.

So we had to act.

I should say that we bore this rat no ill will. He was just part of the fauna that often appeared around the bird feeders in various seasons, along with skunks, possums, chipmunks, and gray squirrels. But in the end, in order to preserve the health of our guardian companion animal, we had to do something.

I set out a live trap, but the rat was too smart to enter. I blocked all the holes that would allow access to the foundation, and jammed the trap in the exit and entrance he appeared to be using. Somehow he got around the obstacle.

I staked the dog near the feeder, which suited him perfectly. He stood guard all day long, staring intently and whining at the rat hole. Which of course alerted the rat that this was not the best of times to come out and feed.

Finally, I gave up and bought a rattrap.

I caught the rat the next morning and immediately regretted what I had done. He was, *enfin*, a healthy wild animal, just trying to get by. Nevertheless I reasoned that we alien Cro-Magnons arrived on these shores ten thousand years before he did and were therefore more native than he—Norway rats did not arrive in the New World until the late seventeenth century.

That was not the end of the dog and rat saga, however. I calculated that our guard needed what human psychologists refer to as "closure." So with the Jack Russell leaping at my waist to get at his prey, I carried the dead rat to a clear spot in the yard, swung him around by his tail, and flung him out across the icy snow. He skidded along as if fleeing, pursued by the dog, who caught him, gave him a death-dealing shake, and tossed him aside—his mission accomplished.

I never told him it was not he who had killed the rat.

※※※※※

The tracks my daughter and I were following that morning soon disappeared in the cover of fluffy snow. But in more sheltered sections of the garden there were signs of the comings and goings of other denizens of the night. A small herd of three or four deer had come out from the woods beyond the western wall, wandered past the greens garden, and in a seemingly formal procession, as if on parade, had marched down the trellis allée and passed on through the yard without stopping to feed on the arborvitae that help define sections of the garden.

Squirrel tracks were everywhere. The little bastings of white-footed mouse tracks threaded here and there in a section of the perennial beds on the western side of the garden, and in front of the house, just below the privet allée, two coyotes passed through.

We also found the single line of tracks of a red fox who had spent a while exploring the garden, stopping periodically to pee, digging here and there in the snow, and trotting on. At one point, it stopped to investigate the signs (some of them invisible to me) left by the other sojourners out on their various forays. And I noticed that the fox halted to seriously consider the footprints of another mammal before moving on—the round tracks of one of my cats, who tend to sleep all day by the woodstove, and then by night revert to their primordial state and set out on night work of their own.

About halfway down the driveway, the two coyotes appeared to have changed their minds, and nosed the tracks of the fox, circled back, and went into the woods at the same place that the fox had come out from. Seeing this I wondered what was beyond, in the dark woods to the southwest, so we crossed the wall and went into the forest. More squirrel tracks everywhere. More mice, one of which seemed to have climbed a tree, and also the double, fluffed-up patch of snow of—I think—a grouse. A fisher had made a dash through the woods and headed down the hill behind the wall to a hollow, where an old deserted carriage road led off to the nearest farm. We saw squirrels again, more mice, a raccoon track, and always here and there along the whole meandering route, the fox, trotting along at a determined pace and threading the whole tapestry of tracks together.

I think I knew this fox. For a while we had a fine little fox family living just behind the garden wall at the edge of the pine stand. Two of the children of the *ladou* came tearing into the house one spring afternoon and whispered dramatically that we must sneak out quietly and see what they had found. There, sleeping in the sun in a nook in the western wall, was a fully furred red fox, her nose tucked beneath her tail. We watched her silently for a while, until at one point she woke and yawned, looked around, and spotted us. She disappeared with such speed that we could not be sure she had even really been there, except that we caught sight of her throughout the spring.

Later we found her den just over the wall, and later still in the season we could see from time to time, if you could get close enough, her four young gray kits. They too would dart away before you could spend any time watching them, though, like puffs of smoke.

We saw Madame Fox, or her husband, Sir Fox, from time to time throughout the season, and we could see often their tracks in winter as they crisscrossed here and there between the walls of the garden and the woods. They were good company, and we missed them when they left for other parts.

The English Lady spotted one of them during one of her

visits, and was surprisingly unimpressed. Foxes have adapted to city life in England and are commonly seen in the tiny gardens of London, and also in the villages such as Royal Tunbridge Wells, and the garden of Jennifer Owen, in Leicester. Our New England red fox—quite fittingly, I suppose, inasmuch as this is the "new" England—has a touch of British red fox in its genes. British foxes were imported here in the eighteenth century, even though there were perfectly good American foxes on the continent, having moved into the region after retreat of the glacier.

Fox lore came along with the British foxes in the form of folktales, most of which portray the wily fox as chicken thief. The favorite around the compound in this regard was Beatrix Potter's *Tale of Jemima Puddle-Duck*, a duck of limited intelligence who one day meets a dashing gentleman with a bushy tail and a red waistcoat who invites her for "dinner" at his house. Foolish duck! She accepts the kind invitation. Fortunately, she is saved at the eleventh hour by the farm dog, Kep, the local collie.

Other fox tales in this country come out of African folklore, some of them preserved in the now-discredited Uncle Remus tales by Joel Chandler Harris. Best known and, in our time, the most controversial of these (there have been a number of political gaffes uttered by various politicians over the years) is the story of the tar-baby, in which the rabbit saves himself by pleading with his captor, the fox, not to throw him into the briar patch.

By contrast, in Japanese folklore, Kitsune, the fox genji, is the trickster, and in some tales, a shape-shifter who can turn himself into a woman. He, or she, is not always the most benign player.

Quite apart from its prominence in folklore, however, a fox was the center of a famous nineteenth-century American court case that helped define the position of private property and ownership in American law. Anyone who has ever studied property law would know the case.

It seems that one fine morning in 1805, a country gentleman named Mr. Lodovick Post set out with his hounds and horse in pursuit of what the law books refer to as a beast *fera natura*, which is to say, a wild animal. The beast in this case was a red fox, an animal despised by Mr. Post—the plaintiff in this particular case—and also by the defendant, a certain Mr. Pierson. In fact, at this point, in contrast to our time, when foxes are generally appreciated, the poor fox was despised by almost everyone, save a few eccentric nature lovers.

The fox in the legal case was regarded by both parties as a pirate, the scourge of barnyards, the bane of farmers, a renegade, a despoiler, an eater of hens. To put him to death, wherever found, was considered meritorious and of public benefit. Accordingly, the law, and also the decision in the case, which ended up as a model legal decision concerning American property rights, offered the greatest possible encouragement to destroy this cunning vandal.

Mr. Lodovick Post had mounted his steed at the crack of dawn on the day in question and with hounds and horn rode out in pursuit of the "wily quadruped"—as the defense termed it. Toward evening, having pursued the windings of Sir Fox the day long, and weary with hunting, Squire Post closed in on his prey, whereupon Mr. Pierson—who had not shared in the labors of the hunt—appeared on the scene. This Pierson, this "saucy intruder," drew his fusil, took aim, shot the fox, and made off with it.

So who owns the fox? Mr. Post, who chased it all day, who tore through brambles, who sweated, who went without lunch, who was stiff with riding, whose hounds were hoarse, breathless, and scratched? Or Mr. Pierson, who happened upon a tired fox and shot it?

Post took Pierson to court, claiming ownership, and won his case. Pierson appealed, and there rose a mighty furor over the poor, long-dead fox, who by this time had been reduced to a pelt. Counsels for both parties reached deep into history to make their points, citing, among others, the Roman emperor Justinian, whose laws held that pursuit alone vests no property. Pierson's counsel argued that the fact that Post rode after the fox all day meant nothing; mere pursuit gave no legal right to ownership. He claimed that the fox became the possession of Pierson as soon as he killed it. Post's counsel countered that whatever Justinian thought about foxes was insignificant. He argued these were modern times (1805!) and society had changed since Roman times, and if society changes, should not also laws change?

Post lost the case, Pierson got his fox after all, and *Pierson v. Post* went on to become a seminal case in the annals of American property law.

But the decision bears watching. In our time, in a world in which "resources" (a loaded, anthropocentric, word if ever there was one) are shrinking, who in fact does own the fox? Sir Fox, were he with us now, would surely argue that he is his own man and beholden to nobody but his wife and little ones.

※※※※※

There was a January thaw later the year of our tracking expedition, around the 12th of the month. Traditionally, this short two- or three-day warming trend occurs around the second week of January. Bees emerge at this time from their hives to take what is known as a cleansing flight; stone flies appear on rocks and tree trunks, soldier beetles can be seen in the crevices of bark, and one might see an occasional early mourning cloak butterfly at this time, as well as chipmunks, skunks, raccoons, and other nonhibernating mammals who lie low during periods of intense cold, and come out to forage when the weather permits.

Everywhere around the larger tree trunks in the garden during these warm halcyon days you can also see the little black dots of snow fleas and springtails. They look like a scattering of pepper. But if you watch carefully, you will see them leap. They belong to an order of primitive, wingless insects called Collembola that have a leg-like device that can hurl them into the air. Also nestled in the deep crevices of bark of the same large trees, you can find the handsome little soldier beetles. They resemble fireflies, but the various species have bright, orderly markings on the backs. They look like well-attired nineteenth-century military figures—thus their common name.

One of the most common mammal signs during these warming trends, and most especially in late winter, are the meandering network of trails made beneath the snow by voles. These appear all around the garden in late winter as the snow begins to melt back. I see them in the snow-covered flower beds, or circling the bird-feeder garden, or proceeding aimlessly across the lawn. The heavy snows were melting that January 12th, and the overhead sun was almost hot in sheltered areas, and everywhere in the snow you could see their little dark lines, about two inches across, running every which way, so dense in some sections that they would cross one another.

The architect of these tunnels, the vole, or meadow mouse, *Microtus pennsylvanicus*, is actually one of the most common mammals in North America, and one of the most prolific. One female may produce some thirteen litters in her one-and-a-half-year life span and, theoretically, could add as many as one hundred new mice to the world in a given year. One single acre of good habitat — that is, an open grassy field — may hold as many as three hundred voles, and possibly more in a good year. As a result, they are considered a pest species in orchards and hayfields. Small though it is, it actually competes with larger domestic mammals as far as forage consumption is concerned.

In spite of this, the vole is also one of the most obscure creatures. Unless you know about them, you are unlikely to see one. They spend virtually all their days feeding on plant material, which they locate at the grassroots level in old fields, meadows, and overgrown lawns. Voles do not hibernate in cold weather but carry on with their activities in burrows just underneath the snow, and because of that, winter is a good time to get a sense of the number of meadow mice that live in any given area. Just go out to a nearby field, or even your own garden, on a warm winter day. If the conditions are warm enough, for long enough to melt the snow down to a few inches above the ground level, you will see their tunnels. They are not unlike the winding tracks of a train yard.

One of the many early commentators on the habits of this

interesting mammal was William Brewster, an old-school field naturalist who carried out his studies a century ago. One February morning Brewster was walking near his farm in Concord, Massachusetts, when he spotted a small, neat hole in a field of otherwise smooth, crusted snow. Around the edges of the hole he noticed the brown fur of a vole and the tracks of a fox. Apparently the passing fox had scented or heard the vole underneath the snow, altered its course, and made a blind dive.

You would think that voles, guarded as they are in the winter by a kindly blanket of snow, would be safe from the myriad enemies who hunt them down from above, that is to say, marsh hawks, red-tailed hawks, kestrels, shrikes, great horned owls, barred owls, long-eared owls, black snakes, milk snakes, weasels, foxes, and fishers, to name but a few. But as Brewster's story makes clear, this is hardly the case. The vole hunters carry on throughout the year.

I once saw the signs of such an attack in a woodland clearing, in the form of a disturbed, scuffed-out section of smooth snow. This was no fox attack; there were no tracks nearby. I did notice, near the scuffling, the imprints of a feathered wing. Apparently an owl had located the mouse beneath the snow simply by listening for it, and then made an accurate dive.

But it is not only predators from above that hunt down the voles in the winter. Vole tunnels become busy highways for animals that live at the ground level, some of which are not averse to eating ("most ungraciously," as Mr. Brewster might have said) the tunnel builders. Moles use the tunnels early and late in the winter, and shrews and weasels burrow through them as well. Shrews tend to be in search of their usual prey, insects and grubs, but they are an opportunistic lot, and the big short-tailed shrew, in particular, will on occasion attack the larger, more cumbersome vole.

Voles can fall victim to almost anything that eats meat, but that fact does not mean that they are passive, roly-poly fellows who plod along through their small, unambitious lives allowing themselves to be eaten without resistance by their myriad enemies. William Brewster once saw a shrike diving repeatedly on something in the snow near his Concord farm. He studied the scene with his field glasses and noticed that the shrike was attacking a vole and that Sir Vole was making a good fight of it. The shrike, a small predatory bird about the size of a mockingbird, was swooping down on the vole and pecking it around the neck. With each attack, the vole rose up on its hind legs and snapped at its predator. After one such attack, presuming itself safe for the moment, the vole turned and headed for its tunnel in the snow. Big mistake. Down swooped the shrike and made a killing hit on the back of the vole's neck.

Voles are rodents, and although they are probably, along with red and gray squirrels, and flying squirrels, among the most common rodents in the garden, they are not alone. There are three, possibly four, species of mouse on this tract of land, the white-footed mouse, the less common house mouse, and the generally rare long-tailed jumping mouse.

I was able to keep track, in a general sort of way, of these various rodent species, because of the cats.

One of these is heavyset and too lazy to hunt, but his brother, the bodhisattva, contrary to his ethereal origins, is a skilled mouser, although, I am happy to say, he is indifferent to bird catching.

Once or twice a week, he generously brings home the remains of his kills, which he consumes on the back porch, leaving a neat pile of innards behind. But sometimes he does not finish his repast, and in this manner, I am able to survey the rodent populations.

His most common catch is the white-footed mouse, which is in fact our greatest pest—every autumn this species moves into the house, bringing in its winter store of nuts and seeds and rattling around the attic and walls all night long. The cat also brings in voles, and the occasional house mouse, which is a somewhat larger, grayer species and favors more urban areas. He also periodically manages to catch a shrew. But two or three times over his life span he has carried home a woodland jumping mouse, an uncommon species—or at least a rarely observed species.

Woodland jumping mice, which vaguely resemble mini kangaroos, live generally in deep forests, and are one of the few species of local mammals, along with the woodchuck and the black bear, that actually hibernate. Most of the other common mammals in North America may disappear in winter, but they do not enter into the death-like torpor of lower body temperature and other physiological states that characterize actual hibernation.

Along with the mice and gray squirrels, the other common mammal in the garden is the cottontail rabbit. For two or three years in the garden I suffered an incursion of these voracious consumers of lettuce and parsley. There were a few rather entertaining rabbits in the first year. We would see them cavorting on the lawn at dusk or feeding peacefully on the white clover I encourage on my greensward. But inasmuch as they were rabbits in the metaphorical as well as the real sense, in spite of the presence of foxes, owls, weasels, and coyotes, and other enemies, there were more the following year, and there was a veritable Normandy invasion the third year.

Rabbits were everywhere, darting away when you went to the compost, or whenever I walked down the drive to get the newspaper or wandered along the garden paths looking for tools or dead-heading flowers. In the second and third year they became seriously destructive. The chard would sprout, put out its first leaves, and the rabbits would move through and decimate it. Replant and they would come again. I tried fences, but they got through. I limited their favorite food plants to one plot, and surrounded it with old windows, and still they got in. I tried to trap them, and they refused to enter the trap. In the end, as with all these natural cycles, their population peaked, and after a curiously benign winter, they disappeared.

The species of rabbit that invaded the garden was the eastern cottontail, which was introduced to the Northeast from the South in the early 1800s. The closely related northern native, the New England cottontail, has been in decline for nearly fifty years and is now considered endangered. Both species need brushy habitats in order to survive, and in fact one of the reasons there were so many rabbits in my garden and not in nearby gardens is that I have encouraged brushy borders, brush piles, and a half-tended wild yard on both my property and my former property down the hill, which is now even more overgrown than when I lived there. Classic rabbit land, in other words.

I have always favored gardens that are rough around the edges, though, and never had a rabbit problem. I suspect one of the reasons that the rabbit population increased so dramatically had to do with my wife's Jack Russell terrier.

He was, as I have suggested, an arch defender of our mutual territory. His work, for which he seemed instinctively trained, was to protect the property from intruders, which, to his dogly mind, were legion. Apart from rabbits and stray cats, there were known to be bears, wolves, foxes, wild ungulates, and all manner of unidentified species lurking in the forest beyond the garden wall. We ourselves could not always see these beasts, and we often wondered why, on some otherwise quiet afternoon, he would charge out through his dog door on the porch and race along the top of the stone wall, barking furiously as if holding at bay a primordial herd of invading mammoths or a rangy pack of dire wolves from the time when this little patch of earth was all heathland and marsh.

One of his archenemies was a train that would pass from time to time on the west side of a lake about a half mile beyond the garden on the northwestern side of Scratch Flat. Whenever he would hear the train whistle, he would charge off the back porch through his door and race out to patrol the walls. He did good work in this regard. No train ever came onto our property.

Often it was not clear why he felt it necessary to sally forth on his defensive skirmishes, but we had a rather fey visitor at the house one afternoon who informed us that dogs can see fairies.

I, of course, reported this important fact to the children.

One afternoon, while I was working in the garden, I heard our defender barking in the woods beyond the back wall. Nothing out of the ordinary really, except that he would return periodically to my side, circle my ankles, and charge out again into the alien forest to resume his barking, which I noticed had a slightly different, more frenetic (if that's possible) timbre to it. It occurred to me that he had treed something, and after a while I went out to see what it was. It turned out he was holding at bay the largest, wildest coyote I have ever seen.

Most of the coyotes that periodically cross through the garden are skittish things that tentatively flit over the walls to feed on compost. If they see you, or hear you, or even think they see you, they fade into the forest. But this animal was a fearless Goliath, and he was standing his ground—a great gray-and-brown-furred, wolf-like thing with a wide head, his forelegs propped on a low rock, staring back at this little canine *poseur* as if to say, You annoying little fice, keep that up and I'm going to do you in. I realized, if he so chose, he could step down and with one snap do away with my loyal companion. So I stepped forward and waved my arms.

Rather than dash away, the coyote merely sauntered off indifferently, took a stand on another boulder, and turned to stare. The dog charged after it, circling and barking with even more ferocity, having presumed, I suppose, that he believed he had got the better of this devil dog. I called him off with a whistle and clapped my hands to scare off the intruder and returned to the garden, the dog at my heels.

We saw this coyote on several occasions after this event. We sometimes saw him standing on a wide stone wall that runs along the west side of the property, the morning sun gleaming off his gray-gold fur. Another time we saw him saunter across the yard, glancing over at the house periodically, straight-legged and spoiling for a fight. He became a commonality. He even earned a name: el Lobo. We actually came to appreciate him for his wildness.

It was about this same time that I learned that his wolf-like appearance was no accident. New genetic studies on the origins of the Eastern coyote seemed to indicate that they were far closer to the original New England wolf, a subspecies of the red wolf, than they were to the simpering little coyotes of the West. He and his like had returned to their native forest habitat along with the bears, fishers, bobcats, white-tailed deer, and other denizens of the primordial forest that grew back in New England after the region lost most of its farmlands.

Twice over the following year, the Jack Russell stood el Lobo off again. Once at the stone wall next to the garden, and once when, for no apparent reason, he appeared in the middle of the vegetable garden among the tomato plants and the chard, glaring back at the house. On both these occasions, alerted by the barking of my assistant, I was the one who ultimately drove him away.

Later that winter, however, there was a third standoff.

As usual we had a big, disorganized group of people at Christmas Eve dinner that year. Late in the evening, one of the guests went out on the porch and found the Jack Russell by the back door, his head hanging low in apparent defeat. He walked in, slowly, an almost unheard-of gait for him, and we noticed that he had a bloodied shoulder and that his unbounded, unstoppable energy seemed to have drained out of him. I gathered him up and found deep bite wounds all around his shoulders.

Within a half an hour we had him bundled up and raced him off to a nearby animal emergency center, which, having determined that he had been badly mauled, sent us off to a nearby university veterinary hospital.

This begat an ironic night drive through the darkened landscape when all the world was stuffed and sleeping off the full dinners of Christmas Eve. The dog was admitted, and the vet, a refined gentleman from one of the southern states, said he was not sure the dog would survive the night.

We drove home and waited for the dreaded call. When it came, around seven, we were informed that he was still alive.

He lived through the second night. The entire staff, having heard his story, began rooting for him. He rallied, lived through the third night, and was released a week later, much battered, barely able to walk, but still counting himself among the living.

At his exit interview from the hospital, the vet explained that he had been picked up and shaken by a large animal, probably a coyote, but that he must have put up a very good fight.

"I imagine," he said in his lazy drawl, "that he must have got in a few good bites."

Maybe he did. After that night, the woods were still. The great horned owls began calling in the hemlock grove in late January. In February the snows began melting back slowly, and by March, the wood frogs began calling from the nearby vernal pool. But we never did see el Lobo again.

The poor dog was never the same after that encounter, though. The drive went out of him, and a year or two later, he gave up and died.

Sic transit gloria mundi, as they used to say. But his death meant an increase in the local rabbit population.

❋❋❋❋❋

I have no documentation of this, but, quite apart from the death of the Jack Russell and the presence of good habitat, I think another reason for the expansion of the rabbit nation was a decline in the local foxes around Scratch Flat. There were foxes elsewhere in the region, according to my naturalist friends, but for some reason they disappeared from the garden the year before the rabbit invasion. Without the centurion guard of an attentive dog, and without any foxes, and an apparently diminished coyote population, perhaps because of the demise of the great wolf-like leader of the pack, the rabbits returned.

Such are the cycles of nature. The foxes increase, so the rabbit population declines. Without rabbits the foxes move on, so the rabbits increase again, and then the foxes come back in force.

I sometimes think of all these denizens of the garden, including the mice, and the foxes, the rabbits, coyotes, voles, shrews, and moles, and the whole company of birds, butterflies, and frogs, as players in some transnational drama in which, in a variation of Shakespeare's phrase, the garden is but a stage for all the natural players of the world. The actors have their exits and entrances, play their parts, and move on.

As one perspicacious ecologist informed me, the same is true of my garden. This too shall pass, as my old mother used to say.

4.

The Bishop's Close

Big firefly:
that way, this way, that way,
and it passes by.

❋ Issa

There is a small garden in Lake Oswego, near Portland,
Oregon, that is known as the Bishop's Close. The garden, which is
no more than six acres or so, sits on a height above the Willamette
River and was laid out by the Olmsted Firm in 1912. In the late
1950s the property was turned over to the bishops of the Diocese
of Oregon, who maintained the garden and eventually opened it
to the public and renamed it the Bishop's Close.

As the English Lady explained on one of her visits, a "close" is
an English term describing an enclosed, cultivated area around an
ecclesiastical building such as a church or chapel, similar to a vicarage garden, but somehow, as I understand it, more formal. The
close outside Portland has a fine island of mixed deciduous trees
near the house, and after I built my little theater set of a garden I
named a section of high trees the Bishop's Close, in honor of the
garden in Oregon.

This garden feature was actually inspired by a stand of the
original native trees on the property. Viewed from the entrance of
the driveway at the lower end of the garden, the Close lies just to

the right of the front of the house, and its main feature is a line of stately red maples that were a part of the original tract and which I had left when I first cleared the land. Eyeing this natural allée time and again as I entered the drive, I (of course) was moved to improve upon it.

Truth be told, in its original natural state it was underlain by thickets of multiflora rose, autumn olive, and the dreaded winged euonymus, or burning bush, and some of the lower limbs of the trees were broken and bent and obscured the view of the house from the road. It did have some fine arching upper limbs that met overhead, however. With a little trimming here and there I managed to create a natural cathedral-like arch of heavy crucks supporting a roof of leafy branches that framed the house on the hill. I then went to work and cleared the understory and then forged on and planted a mix of native and nonnative trees on the outer boundaries of the grove.

The Close now has, interspersed with a backdrop of arborvitae, a row of katsuras, rough bark maples, stewartias, white birches, dogwoods, and Japanese maples on the sides, and, at the end nearest the house, a planting of Lombardy poplar, dawn redwood, larch, a weeping katsura, and a ginkgo tree.

All this is further accentuated by an allée of privet that I planted as a boundary for the rough mead that sweeps from the road up to the gabled front of the house. But its main feature is more obscure, namely the life forms that have moved into the Close since it was fashioned.

I keep the interior of the Close clear of undergrowth; it now consists of a floor of rough native grasses that I mow periodically with a scythe. In spring, this semi-shaded interior and the half-tended grasses around the Close sprout a fine crop of wildflowers. The weedy edges and the interior are a favorite spot for what are known as stridulating insects—that is, crickets, grasshoppers, and katydids—that sing nightlong in the proper season.

The season of insect song begins in early April, when I hear the first tentative tiny bells and then the chirps and trills of the meadow crickets. This sound increases through the spring and summer and continues well into the fall, after the populations have increased sufficiently. The crickets create a sustained, high-pitched ringing, a sound that is so ever present it becomes white noise. No one who is unfamiliar with meadow crickets hears it unless I point the sound out to them.

Later in the spring, I begin to hear field crickets, the larger black to light brown crickets that traditionally move into houses each autumn and hang out around the hearths in living rooms and country kitchens. They are native to Europe but have become well established in this country. In our time, with screen doors, and the sealed walls, doors, and windows of contemporary houses, such as those in the Quail Hollow Estates, this pleasing country tradition is fast dying out. But field crickets still make it into my house, I am happy to report; in fact, I encourage them. Like good old-fashioned crickets of folklore, they seem to favor the area around the woodstove, probably because it is warm, and because the wood I stack there offers them shelter. I often leave crumbs around their hangouts just to keep them fed. I can sometimes hear them chirping even on snowy January nights.

Also in early summer in the Close, the Carolina grasshoppers appear; these are large, flighty grasshoppers with striped wings that scatter ahead of me whenever I mow. They sound off with a shushing sort of rattle as they fly away. As the season progresses, their populations grow. So do the populations of the cone-headed grasshoppers, which add their songs to the night chorus. But in my opinion, the finest of all the various cricket songs do not join the chorus until mid-July. That is when I begin to hear the ringing of the snowy tree crickets, a light-colored climbing insect that hangs out on low-growing shrubs.

These too are ubiquitous, but rarely noticed by those who don't know what to listen for. They produce a mid-toned bell-like chirp that, as far as I can tell, is pitched close to G-flat on a piano, although when it gets hot they seem to rise a half tone or so. Groups of them will gather in the same plant among nearby shrubs and in hedges, and when they hear one another singing, they will chirp in unison, producing an intense throbbing sound like a heartbeat, which on hot summer nights can be quite loud. It's a beautiful, sultry sound that reminds me of mint juleps and nights on the Eastern Shore of Maryland where my family used to gather each summer. I believe it must have been the snowy tree cricket that Hawthorne was referring to when he wrote the phrase "If moonlight could be heard, it would sound like that."

Like all insects, snowy tree crickets are responsive to ambient temperatures; they slow down or speed up depending on the weather, so that you can actually get a sense of degrees a thermometer would register by listening to their calls. There is even a general formula for this related to snowy tree crickets. In fact there are many formulas, but the easiest one is to count the number of beats in fifteen seconds and then add forty.

By late August the night orchestra reaches full crescendo when the tree-dwelling katydids begin to sing. Katydids seem to prefer old oak trees as a habitat, and there are not many oak trees around the garden, let alone in the Close, where most of the stridulating insects in this garden gather. There are a few oaks on the periphery, however, where the katydids seem to collect, and these we can hear on warm August nights from the back porch during late dinners.

There used to be a restaurant over a pond in a nearby town that had a good population of katydids. You could come out after dinner and be nearly deafened by their calling. As is often the case in these situations, even the sober few who would emerge after dinner would fail to hear them unless I happened to point them out. Most people appreciate the information, but I have occasionally had an unfriendly or mystified reaction. One large gentleman, cut in the style of a football player, widened his eyes when I mentioned them and asked if they sting. Another intense, wiry little man told me he knew all about them. "I hate those things," he said.

Cricket song notwithstanding, the insect of the Close that has generated the most entertainment among the compound children are the lightning bugs that appear in late June and flicker through the night. There are several species of these insects in the Close and the nearby garden beds and the grasses of the mead, and each species is active at different times of the night. They also fly at different heights, some low to the ground, or even down in the grasses, and some fly high above the tree line, or drift across open areas at mid-level, flashing lazily. Each species has its own flash patterns and flying patterns, and I learned that these may be further divided by the sexes. The males are the high fliers, the females lay low near the ground and flash to attract the males.

Although I believe, with the increase in local insecticides and the general cleanliness of suburban yards, coupled with what seems to be a fear of the outdoors among suburbanites, the tradition is now in decline, catching lightning bugs in a clear jar was one of the prime entertainments of summer nights. I spent a great deal of my youth chasing them (along with other insects, bats, snakes, frogs, muskrats, and tadpoles), and I have encouraged night hunts among the various generations of the children of the garden.

Fireflies have had a long history of folkloric attraction. My father lived in China and Japan for three years, and while he was there (or maybe before he went out), he developed an interest in Eastern folklore and the work of the Irish American writer Lafcadio Hearn, who took on Japanese citizenship and collected together the dispersed folktales of Japan in various books. Fireflies were popular in Japanese culture, there are still firefly festivals, and there were many firefly folktales, one of which was the story of Princess Firefly. I remember the tale from summer nights on my family's farm on the Eastern Shore of Maryland.

Sometimes on hot nights when the river winds were still and the smell of the surrounding fields would curl around the house, we would all sit on the west porch and watch the fireflies rise over the hayfields above the river. The air was thick then, and summer had its grip on us, and sometimes it would seem that the very house would lift from its foundation and float suspended above the ground, amid the blinking flashes of the fireflies and the dark surround of the cedar trees and the black fields.

On such a night, when the adult conversation slowed, some-one—usually a kid—would ask my father to tell again the story of Princess Firefly and why moths and beetles seek light.

The story, retold in the rambling, easygoing southern narrative style of my father, involved a beautiful princess. Never mind that she was a firefly, in the kingdom of the insects she was the most beautiful in the land and all the swains adored her. Her parents wanted her to marry, and in fact there was no lack of suitors. Each night, splendidly attired beetles in shining armor arrived at her court along with princely lacewings in delicate netted coats and velvet-cloaked moths and, most elaborate of all, butterflies in all manner of brightly colored ceremonial capes and robes.

She refused them all.

As the years passed, her parents grew concerned that she would never marry. Each spring they would insist that she accept one of them, and each year, she was unable to make up her mind. Finally, in order to please her parents and put an end to the matter, she announced that she would marry that insect who could best match her own brilliance.

One after another, the suitors took up the challenge. Great bronze-backed June bugs flew off into the surrounding country-side of the kingdom to find light. The silent moths flitted through the darkness of the fields, lacewings and crane flies circled through the world searching for a firelight to bring back to the princess at her court.

As they searched through the land they noticed, seemingly for the first time, the bright gleams of the oil lamps of country people shining in the night. Here was the night fire they sought, and they circled round and round, drawn to the brightness on the dark world of night. Some grew brave and dashed into the fire, singeing their wings. Some simply collected near the light, planning, and some only waited nearby. But try as they might, not one could capture a fire so marvelous as that of the princess. They refused to give up, though, and to this day, they still collect around outdoor lamps.

The princess never did marry.

This, perhaps needless to say, was a story I related to the two generations of children that grew up, or are still growing up, on the compound.

I remember that there was always a slow silence after my father completed his firefly tale. Beyond the porch the river turned black, the bright flashes of light flickered over the field. No one spoke. I remember the rhythmic creak of the rockers on the splintery porch floor, bullfrogs bellowing from the frog pond behind the main house, the *quock* of the night herons down on the dark riverbank, the sultry air, and below the house, like Japanese lanterns, the dancing of the lights of ten thousand fireflies.

And all around the oil lamps on the porch, flitting and circling in the dark surround, I could see lacewings, and beetles and white-cloaked moths, still hopeful after all these centuries.

Often on those hot nights, as children have done for a thousand years, my cousins and I would descend from the porch with kitchen jars and sweep the grasses, catching the flashers and carrying them around in the jars like mystic lanterns.

Timing seemed everything to me, even then. Why did the fire-flies flash at certain intervals? Why did they quit flashing periodically, and why did some of them never take to the air and stay low in the grasses, emitting a long, sustained light?

It was only later that I learned that there was a dark side to the luminous display taking place in the fields below the house, and that all the bright poetic legends and folktales had an element of truth. Out there in the real world of the grassroot jungle, the lights that so inspired the folktales and festivals were all about sex and death.

Fireflies flash to attract mates, and it is for the most part the males that we see on summer nights. Shortly after they reach adulthood, usually around late June, as dusk falls, the males launch themselves in the air and patrol to and fro across open areas, flashing a semaphoric signal to female fireflies, who lie below, watching. There are as many as thirty different species of firefly, and the males of each species have a set pattern of flashes, which the female of the species can recognize.

Below in the grasses, females spotting a potential mate light up with a sustained flash. The male blazes back, the female lights up again, and, after a series of exchanges, the male descends to locate his mate. Sometimes more than one suitor will fly down, and the firefly princess will be surrounded by a company of suitors, each flashing handsome signals. But fireflies, it appears, are discreet denizens of this untamed, complex world. Once the couple has found each other the lights go out and they mate.

All is not love in the world of fireflies, however; there is also the question of sustenance. There is one species of firefly that makes use of the flashing repertoire of males to attain a meal. These carnivorous *femmes fatales* lie low in the grass and watch for the signals of other species of males flashing above. They imitate the flash pattern and draw the unsuspecting male down to his demise.

But all that is science. When you are ten years old, and it is night, and the sparking stars of fireflies drift over the hay fields, and the wind is in the corn, it is all a half-lit poetic mystery.

※※※※※

Just south of the Close, running from the front of the house down to a curved hedge of hemlocks at the base of the hill, is a long narrow *prato*, or mead, a design element I stole from the Villa Farnesina, in Rome. Here, on sunny days, another favorite insect of Japanese folktales crisscrosses the yard—the famous *tombo*, or dragonfly.

Except for a few obvious species, this is another one of those families of insects that requires the work of a specialist to identify individuals properly. Among other problems, in order to study them you have to catch them, and they are notoriously fast fliers. Nonetheless, I have what the English Lady might term a number of Odonata aficionados among my friends, and they have spotted, although not positively identified, at least ten different species casting about in the circular space at the end of the privet allée. Some of these I was familiar with, some I believe are worldwide in distribution, and may be the same as the species that occur in the various Japanese folktales and poems concerning dragonflies.

Here, and especially over the insect-haunted flower beds in

summer, I commonly see red meadowhawks, green darners, and ten-spots, all of which are species that spend part of their time inland. Many dragonflies spend their season of life around streams and ponds, and all of them begin their lives in water. The eggs are deposited on the surface of still waters and drift to the bottom. They eventually hatch into hideous and dangerous-looking predatory nymphs that cling to rocks and sandy bottoms, feeding on smaller aquatic beetles and bugs, including other dragonfly nymphs. They may spend as many as four years in this stage, and then, one still night in summer, propelled by whatever internal mechanisms drive nymphs to become adults, they climb up a plant stem and, over the course of a night, work their way out of their former watery lives to spend the rest of their days casting about as dragonflies in the upper airs.

Among the most obvious and interesting of these is the green darner.

If you live near grassy meadows or open fields, a golf course, or even if you have a large lawn, and you watch the sky above these open areas from midmorning to dusk, you may see the darting forms of these big dragonflies zipping to and fro. It is one of the larger species of dragonfly, and has clear wings, and if you can get close enough you will see that it has a black spot in front of its eyes.

Unlike most other dragonflies, in fact unlike most insects, green darners migrate, and late summer and early autumn is the time to watch for them. Like other migratory species, birds and monarch butterflies, they take advantage of clear days with a northwest wind to move; on a warm afternoon, you can sometimes see hundreds of these handsome insects darting across fields and meadows and along beaches. They appear to move in groups—if you see one, you are likely to see many. I once counted ten green darners zipping to and fro over the mead between the porch and the Lady Garden, a little like a flock of feeding swallows.

Once in the South (no one is certain exactly where they go), they breed, lay their eggs, and die. After hatching, the newly emerged nymphs spend three or four years in the nymph stage. Following this period, they metamorphose and the southern brood of adults emerges and begins, in the spring, a northward migration.

✳✳✳✳✳

Of all the cultures in the world, no doubt the Japanese have the most literature and art devoted to insects, and of all the insects to choose from, a vast body of literature and scroll paintings is devoted to dragonflies. Part of this may be due to the fact that Japan has more than two hundred species of dragonfly; it is—or was, at least—what one writer called the El Dorado of neuropteran fanciers. In fact, one of the early names for Japan was *Ahitsushima*, or Land of the Dragonfly.

The legend holds that two thousand years ago the emperor Jimmu ascended a mountain to view the province of Yamato. He thought the land took on the shape of a dragonfly licking its tail, and eventually the whole island was so named. Another legend holds that a dragonfly swept down and ate a horsefly that was biting the emperor's arm and he named the country in its honor.

My father was so taken with the works of Lafcadio Hearn that he wrote his graduate thesis on Hearn's mysticism and collected all of his published books, which I inherited after he died. It seems that Lafcadio himself was interested in dragonflies. He used to catch them and identify them, and he devoted a chapter of one of his books to the Japanese lore of Odonata.

In Lafcadio's time—the late nineteenth century—dragonfly catching was still a favorite pastime of children, and there are vast numbers of haiku picture poems devoted to dragonflies, not to mention scroll paintings. The great nineteenth-century painter Hokusai has a little-known sketchbook depicting many of the different species.

In order to help with his translation of the dragonfly folklore, Hearn includes a section in his book on dragonfly identification, including illustrations, and the beautiful, sometimes odd names of the common species of *tombo,* or トンボトンボ. The only ones I was able to recognize were the *Ko-Mugi-tombo,* or wheat straw dragonfly, which I believe must be our ten-spot dragonfly, and the *Kino Tombo,* or yellow dragonfly, probably our wandering glider, a species that is found on every continent except Antarctica. The others, although possibly endemic only to Japan, have elaborate, beautiful names, such as the Shining Loins Dragonfly or the Dragonfly of the Ancestral Spirits, and the Ghost Dragonfly.

I have had help catching butterflies with one of the youngest members of the compound, and periodically we have gone after dragonflies as well, usually without much success. But we could have learned something from the techniques of Japanese children. Dragonflies mass in late summer and early autumn in Japan, just as they do here, and late summer was the catching season in Japan.

Children would smear birdlime on the end of bamboo poles and wait for dragonflies to land. They would sometimes use nets, and sometimes swat them with a light pole—although killing one or maiming one was thought to bring on bad luck. The most interesting method was to catch a female and fasten a thread to her tail tied to a long light stick. The children would then allow the dragonfly to circle, and soon a male would descend to mate and attach himself. The two of them would then be drawn down. Children could catch eight or ten males with a single female by this means. They also used to make a mini bolo with a strand of long hair with two small pebbles at either end. They would throw the bolos into the air in areas where dragonflies were hunting, and the dragonflies would dive at one of the pebbles, mistaking them for prey, and become entangled.

I tried this method once with my assistant dragonfly catcher, who was all of five years old at the time. We used a strand of my wife's long hair, affixed pebbles to the ends, and cast the bolo above one of the flower beds. We missed with the very first shot, and had to spend another five minutes looking for our bolo. We tried another two or three times, and finally lost the bolo somewhere in the depths of a hydrangea and gave up.

I wonder sometimes why Asian cultures have developed such an appreciation for insects. In Europe, dragonflies are viewed as agents of the devil—evil beings who sting horses and torture people. The related damselflies or darning needles that inhabit ponds and lake edges were thought to sew shut the mouths and eyes of children who lie to their parents.

Crickets, admittedly, have a better reputation in Western culture; the cricket on the hearth is a favorite image in English romantic poetry. But they come nowhere near the favor that crickets have achieved in Japanese culture. Crickets appear in haiku poetry almost as frequently as dragonflies. Traditional haiku poems require a reference to a season, and the mention of a cricket always symbolized autumn.

Lafcadio Hearn includes cricket lore in his various writings, including the popularity of crickets as pets. They were so popular that people would breed them and sell them at markets. Hearn reports accounts of a thriving cricket trade as far back as the seventeenth century. He also cites the earliest accounts of cricket hunting. It appears in the first-century Japanese classic *The Tale of Genji*, although poetry involving crickets reaches back even farther.

The Japanese appreciation for crickets was actually imported from China, where cricket lore was even stronger and appears earlier. Crickets have been kept as pets in China for thousands of years, and were even used in the cricket equivalent of cockfights, with victorious cricket individuals progressing upward through more and more battles. A good fighting cricket could sell for the equivalent of one hundred dollars or more, and there are records of bets made on cricket battles that range in the equivalent of thousands of dollars. Great fighting crickets, known as Generals, were laid to rest after their demise in tiny silver coffins.

The Chinese bred crickets, but they also ranged through the countryside to catch more pets to bring into the cricket markets. There are records of cricket hunts from 742 AD, describing ladies of the palace catching crickets in little golden cages. There was even a literary work devoted to the cricket, *The Book of Crickets*, written by the minister of state Kia Se-tao, published in the thirteenth century.

Wandering down the privet allée on hot summer nights, surrounded by the cacophony of clicks, buzzings, chirps, and tiny silver bells of all the stridulating insects of the Close, I sometimes like to imagine one of our heads of state authoring such a book; the US attorney general publishing a field guide to the damselflies of the Northeast, perhaps, or *Field Crickets in Lore and Literature* by the American secretary of state.

Unfortunately, all this Eastern insect lore and admiration stands out in marked contrast to the indifference, lack of appreciation, and even disgust that is afforded to this rich culture of living things by our people in our time and place.

❋❋❋❋❋

By late September and the first chill nights, the full chorus of singing insects begins to wane. I've never documented this, but it seems to me that the first to fall silent are the grasshoppers. Then as the nights grow cooler, the katydids slow to a rhythmic dirge. The beat of the snowy tree crickets decreases, and one by one, like the musicians in Haydn's "Farewell Symphony," the insect musicians slowly depart from the stage, and soon a winter silence will envelop the land.

5.

The Lady Garden

How could such sweet and wholesome hours
Be reckoned but with herbs and flowers!

✳ Andrew Marvell

As the wedding plans developed, I began the process of digging out new beds for annuals, and replanting and transplanting some of the tired old perennials and shrubs. I had, all told, seven different flower beds around the property. Some of these were solely perennial borders, some were a mix of annuals and perennials, some consisted mainly of herbs, and all of them were in sorry shape compared to other flower gardens I know. I lived with this dilemma, knowing that I probably had too many beds to maintain and that some of these were not in the best possible sites for the kind of flowers I wanted to grow. With the advancing wedding date, I felt I should make a semblance of an attempt to formalize them somewhat and lay on an illusion of order.

The wedding itself was planned to take place in a stand of hemlocks about two hundred yards inside a deciduous forest owned by Mr. Findlay. But there was to be a brief announcement of the wedding plans delivered from the porch of the Swan Cottage for the assembled. In order to make room for the wedding guests at the site, I mowed down a plot of native wild grass and ground covers under a hickory grove on the southeast side of the cottage, and dug out a new flower bed on the northeast side. I then began working on a series of beds in the circular border at the edge of the lawn on the south side of the house, which, with its screened porch, glassed-in dining room, and many-windowed living room, is the main living quarters of the house.

At the time I was in the process of carrying out these works, the English Lady arrived for a visit.

Mrs. Theodosia Huntingfield of Royal Tunbridge Wells dresses in subdued tweeds with a fine golden thread and sensible shoes. She wears a short-brimmed trilby hat and traditional green Wellingtons in cloudy weather and walks around the garden sniffing flowers, inspecting buds, and deadheading annuals as if she were the head gardener here. The English Lady, it must be said, does not approve of flashy, hot tropical colors in a flower bed. No begonias, alyssums, marigolds, salvias, aubrietia, nor any astilbes, and certainly no garden *arrivistes* such as pampas grass. She does permit hollyhocks, as well as clematis and old-fashioned roses, also lupines, delphiniums, and peonies. But no bright orange, or yellows, and never any garish reds such as the blaze roses that ascend the east wall of my garage. She favors the subdued colors of Renaissance paintings, hellebores and euphorbias, lavender, but not the fancy sort, the standard, with a good strong scent. "Sweet peas, violets, sweet William, and foxglove, preferably white," she says. "No asters, nor any chrysanthemums, and roses only in pale pink. And no modern hybrids; they must be sweet-scented, densely petaled, and if they climb—well, all the better."

Although that, generally speaking, does not match exactly my own philosophy of flower plantings, I like the idea.

But not entirely.

By contrast my wife, Jill, better known as JiJi by the younger set of the *ladou*, is more of an Impressionist when it comes to garden palettes. She likes the colors of hot climates, of Monet, Van Gogh, and Matisse, along with strong drafts of the warm Côte d'Azur. She believes in companion planting and puts circles of bright marigolds around her tomato plants. She favors masses of color, rather than single, rare plants. Provençal yellows, lavenders, pale blues, but no strong reds, and she barely tolerates the oranges of my daylilies. She carries home flats of annuals, which I dutifully plant, only to have them dug up and replanted elsewhere by her because the colors clash with the house or with each other, or because they will clash at some future point when some nearby blooming shrub bursts into flower. The house is peach-colored, with white trim. No strong reds permitted.

Inside the house, the glassed-in dining room matches her garden style. The shelves and walls are decorated with Deruta plates from Umbria, faience, Spanish tiles, and Portuguese azulejos she has collected on her various overseas garden sojourns. I saw once in an old *National Geographic* magazine the interior of a traditional gypsy wagon. It looked very much like our dining room.

The English Lady takes tea in this sun-filled conservatory and does not comment.

The two of them go around the garden chatting amicably about children and dogs and sniffing flowers—a Renaissance figure out of a Botticelli painting, with golden locks and dressed in lavender and rose, and an angular *Anglaise* in a tweed skirt, with graying, straight-cut hair.

But in spite of the fact that I am in agreement with Madame Theodosia Huntingfield's taste in perennials, there is something to be said for the hot annuals of JiJi's flower beds—for one thing, they attract bees and butterflies and hummingbirds.

Even before the remake in preparation for the wedding, the beds had their own populations of insects and mammalian herbivores, such as meadow mice, rabbits, and chipmunks. I had planted one garden bed—known as the Lady Garden because of a fanciful birdbath held up by the three half-clad Graces—specifically to attract butterflies, moths, and hummingbirds. It took a while to fill out, but in the second year, the colorful denizens of concentrated patches of echinacea, buddleias, roses, daisies, salvias, bergamot, and a flowering hyssop assumed full bloom.

Early in the spring, the dark-purple mourning cloaks would emerge from beneath the bark and boards where these unique hibernating butterflies wintered over. They will sometimes appear as early as February, and one year I saw one in the garden during the January thaw. Following the mourning cloaks, the thumbnail-sized spring azures appear, and will remain in the garden over the spring and summer, passing through many generations. The late-summer individuals are paler than the early-spring generation. After that, the full contingent of seasonal butterflies moves in, each in its appointed time, the viceroys, the banded purples, tiger swallowtails, black swallowtails, red admirals, fritillaries, the yellow sulfurs, and finally, the lords of them all, the well-known and popular monarchs, which along with the green darners are one of the few migratory insects.

Each autumn from the plains of Canada, from the cornfields

of Iowa, the meadows of Ohio, the hilltown fields and forgotten overgrown pastures of New England, from every uncut lawn and lot throughout the eastern half of North America, the monarch butterflies set out for the high valleys and slopes of Michoacán, in the highlands of central Mexico.

Here, in the mountain fastness and the rich oyamel fir forests, they spend the winter, clustered together on the tree branches, millions upon millions of them, so thick they festoon the trees with color.

For the following two to three months, throughout the vagaries of weather, through cold snaps, snowstorms, hurricanes, and rains, they wait, until the lengthening light and warming days and some as-yet-ill-understood trigger in their tiny insect wiring indicates that it is time to set out for the North.

Even though this impressive southward migration is one of the most stressful events in the life of a monarch butterfly, in evolutionary terms it must have been worth the trip. For the past eight thousand years, ever since the northern sections of North America were free of glacial ice and suitable for deciduous plants, the mountain slopes of Michoacán have provided a winter sanctuary for these butterflies.

※※※※※

The caterpillars of the various species of butterflies of my garden each has its favorite food plants, most of which, partly by design, but generally by accident, I have growing in the garden. The black swallowtail, for example, favors parsley, so I always allow a patch to grow up to full flower. Monarchs love milkweed, fritillaries love violets, the sulfurs love clover, and viceroys love willow, plum, cherry, and apple—and they all of them love color. On still, hot summer afternoons, they virtually dance over the asclepias, buddleias, and coneflowers that grow in the various flower beds. Skippers, which are halfway between moths and butterflies, also dash about everywhere in certain seasons, and there are any number of moths, including the large hummingbird moth that feeds in the flower beds just off the back porch on the same flowers as the hummingbird itself.

In the early years of this garden, I rarely saw that other denizen of flower beds, the hummingbirds, except in September, when they would begin migrating through the area. But as the perennial beds increased and I began using more annuals, hummingbirds began to nest somewhere on the property. Hummingbird feeders help make them more visible, but almost any day in the garden I will see them among the flowers.

One year, after hummingbirds began to nest somewhere around the garden (I never could find their nests) I discovered an interesting alternative to hummingbird feeders. I was watering the garden one summer morning when a hummingbird sped out of nowhere and began flying to and fro in the plume of spray. I held the hose steady and the bird halted in midair, fluttering. I realized it was probably enjoying a bath. Since then, I sometimes go out purposely to water, just to bring out the hummingbirds. Wherever they are waiting, they are very alert to the presence of spraying water, possibly because of the colors of refracted light from the spray.

One morning I was using a watering can and one appeared and sped to and fro through the stream, no more than a foot from my knee.

My other flower beds were not necessarily designed to attract butterflies; they are, generally speaking, random plantings of flowers that are given to me, or that family members or guests bring in. But any random garden can be easily created to attract hummingbirds with bright colors.

By midsummer, when the annuals are in full swing, the flowers are also alive with the hum and buzz of an energetic feeding frenzy of insects. Big heavy-bodied bumblebees and honeybees crowd in, along with the smaller sweat bees and mason bees, as well as a host of species of flies, beetles, ants, and buzzing things I can hardly see to identify. Passing near one of the hydrangeas on a hot summer afternoon, you couldn't miss the fact that there are heady flowers nearby, even if you were blind; the noise level of these frenetic feeders is intense. So is the smell of the hydrangeas, a certain musky odor that is distinctive, as far as I can tell, to hydrangeas.

Here too among the flowers of full summer, I always find the finely crafted little crab spiders, who lurk just under the flower heads. Some of these are pure white, with a hint of yellow, some are gray, with a camouflaging pattern of black stripes and dots, and all of them blend exquisitely with the flowers beneath which they hide. Crab spiders—so named because they do in fact resemble colorful mini-crabs—do not construct webs. They lay in wait and then ambush their prey. Although they will take beneficial insects, such as the bees and wasps, they will also control pest species, such as thrips, and certain species of moths. Some of them, the golden-rod spider, for example, can change color, ranging from the bright yellows of goldenrods to a pale white.

Moths also appear in the flower beds in the height of summer, but many of these species are night fliers and take over the work of pollination after the sun has set. Unlike butterflies and skippers, moths have feathered antennae, and unlike butterflies, they depend on scent to identify flowers, rather than sight. The feathers of the antennae help pick up the odors. Some of these night fliers are among the crown jewels of the full-winged tribe of this order of insects.

One night, lounging on the back porch after dinner, someone spotted a pale greenish thing that looked like a stray piece of paper against the dark backdrop of the woods wall. It seemed tossed by the wind, except that there was no wind that still June night, and the paper had the ability to move upward. I knew instantly what had come, and raced out the back door. It was the prized luna moth, a giant lime-green moth that generally emerges from its pupa in the morning, flutters around the countryside for a week or so seeking a mate, consummates its marriage, and then dies. Beautiful though it is, it is rarely seen, since it generally flies at night and lives only one week.

Other giant moths in this group include the huge one-eyed (seemingly) Polyphemus moth, a brown- to cinnamon-colored moth that lives in woodlands. I can't remember seeing one of these around the garden over the years, although they do occur in the nearby woods.

Some of the moths that move into the flower gardens, in particular the cabbage moths, which appear in spring, are considered pests. But the fluttering white cabbage moths are a common sight above the spring garden and, their feeding habits notwithstanding, I like them. They remind me of the white-sailed skiffs of sailing schools tacking around colorful buoys.

Also in spring and through the summer, along with the mourning cloaks and spring azures, I see the fast-flying little skippers. These are a family of butterflies but have a few significant differences. Unlike the flitting, bouncing flight of a monarch or a swallowtail, the skippers dash about the garden in fast, darting flights. They are actually a rather large family, with over three thousand or so species worldwide, but they are generally overlooked even by garden lovers who enjoy, but may not know, the various species of butterflies that appear in their gardens. If you can manage to catch a skipper, they are easy to identify as such; just look at the antennae. Butterflies have little clubs at the end of their antennae. Skippers do too, but the clubs are smaller and angle backwards, a little like putting clubs. They also have rather plump bodies, and shorter, more powerful wings. Beyond that, identifying the species within the family is not easy. Even entomologists have a problem and need microscopes to properly determine which species is which. The only one I have been able to positively identify is the silver-spotted skipper. I know these because they favor wisteria, which I have growing in various sites around the gardens.

It would take a serious insect survey to actually determine the number of different insects that appear in this garden. My general records of the living things have been carried out at a larger scale, following the taxonomic system that begins with the kingdom, as in animal or plant, and then moves on down the line, through phylum, class, order, family, genus, and species. I know there are many more insect families—let alone genera and species—that occur here whose identities are totally mysteries to me than ones I am able to recognize. But occasionally I have become obsessed with determining who's who.

When I lived in the Swan Cottage, for example, I was beset on late summer nights by some annoying tapping and fluttering noises around the ceilings of the cottage. It turned out to be a certain species of brown moth; probably, I thought, a noctuid moth, which generally flies at night. I caught one and spent hours trying to figure out what it was. I eventually determined that it was probably something called an American copper underwing moth. I read that they tend to flock together, which explains why there were so many inside the cabin. Clearly, I had set up house in their territory.

I have also had some serendipitous good luck with lesser-known insects. One day I had a very long conversation with a naturalist friend about an insect known as the phantom crane fly, an uncommon genus of crane flies, which themselves are not so common. Crane flies often make their way into people's houses in the summer and are—unfortunately—often swatted even though they are harmless, because they resemble huge mosquitoes. Some species such as the phantom crane fly may not even eat during its short life span, and certainly does not sting.

The phantom crane fly, I learned, is so named because it has the unique ability to disappear in midflight. This is achieved because their striped legs have a pattern of black and white so that when they fly against a shaded or half-lit background, the alternating pattern of black and white makes them seem to disappear altogether. They are not strong fliers; in fact, they look like pieces of fluff drifting through the air.

I was having a drink on the back porch that very evening and saw a piece of fluff drift over the Lady Garden. Suddenly the fluff disappeared. I snatched up a butterfly net, raced outside, and when the fluff appeared again, snagged it. There were the telltale striped legs, the large mosquito shape and all—the infamous phantom, trapped at last.

Actually, the fact that I caught one on the very day that I learned of their existence says something, I think, about the nature of the world around us. You have to wonder if you cannot see that which you don't know exists. Which in turn says something about learning to see. Which further says something about an educational system that relies on electronic media, books, and a national school system that takes place indoors in brightly lit, climate-controlled, ugly rooms. Old William Wordsworth summed up the situation. One impulse from a vernal wood taught him more of good and evil than all the sages could, as he pointed out in his poem "The Tables Turned."

I think of the poor, deprived children of the Quail Hollow Estates. I know they are in there somewhere in their mausoleums, because I have seen them waiting for their enclosed school buses on weekday mornings to be carried off to their enclosed schoolrooms, in school systems that are cutting the already short, twenty-minute outdoor recesses because of budgetary constraints. On sunny Saturday mornings in fall and spring and summer, the children are nowhere to be seen. And when they do appear outdoors, as the children of one or two of the twenty or so houses in the development do, they are hard at work at sport practice.

Not to harp on my useful foil, the Quail Hollow Estates; the people who live there are perfectly friendly, hardworking families. But I can't help but notice that even on sunny days, some mothers actually drive their children no more than one hundred yards or so to wait for their school buses in either heated or air-conditioned cars. I sometimes have to wonder what hope can there be for such a people!

※※※※※

This idea of not being able to see that which you do not know exists got me thinking about what else there is in the Vicarage Garden that I have not been able to take into account in my decades of rambles through the wilderness of my own backyard. With that in mind, I have periodically invited various true-to-form naturalists into the garden to see what they could see and I could not.

One of the oddest—and also most productive—of these expeditions was an adventurous journey to look for fungi in the most unlikely month of the year for an assessment of living things— January, the traditional Hunger Moon of the local Eastern Woodland native cultures.

I had a general idea of which mushrooms were growing around the grounds in the various seasons. I had found most of the common ones, such as puffballs, oyster mushrooms, meadow mushrooms, and honey mushrooms. Periodically, in season, I gather these edible species for dinner or for entertainment. The most popular mushroom among the younger set, for example, is the fairy ring mushroom, *Marasmius oreades*.

Other species of mushrooms may grow in rings. The phenomenon occurs when the mycelium, which is the actual vegetative part of the fungus, grows ever outward, seeking nutrients. The mushrooms, the things we normally see, are the fruiting bodies of the plant, and they spring up in a circle when they fruit.

But that is only one version of the explanation for the appearance of the fairy ring. The other, which is by now well known to the children of the garden (among many others, and for many centuries), is the fact that the ring marks the place where fairies held a circle dance the night before.

During my mushroom-hunting forays around the garden I have had some happy surprises. Elsewhere on the compound, I once found a fine stand of morels. They appeared for several years running in an area where an old apple tree had once stood, and then just as abruptly disappeared.

I also found nearby a false morel, a known poisonous species. I noticed it and realized it was not your average morel, but I didn't have my mushroom book on hand that day and was thinking about eating it. Morels are, of course, among the most sought-after of the edible mushrooms. Collectors who have located a patch generally kept the location to themselves. Fortunately, I knew enough not to tempt fate, and waited to make an accurate identification. And in fact it did turn out to be a poisonous false morel.

Also on the compound grounds, but not technically in my garden, I have found a fine stand of wine caps. These I consumed for several years until for some reason they failed to appear. Wine caps tend to appear in late summer, sometimes even earlier, and are marked by their brown to wine-red caps and violet gills and are fairly easy to identify and not uncommon. One year I fed on them regularly, a little like a lettuce crop.

Unfortunately, after one fine repast of wine caps, I woke up early in the night feeling rather ill. All imaginary, I thought. I am hardly scientific in my mushroom identification, and periodically, after consuming a dish, I begin to wonder if I remembered to check the gill pattern, or the spore color, or whether there were any deadly amanitas disguised and hiding in among the young puffballs I had gathered. I end up waiting for the next six hours to see whether I am going to die of mushroom poisoning.

Partly because of my unorganized, unscientific collecting habits, I have had a healthy suspicion of mushroom poisoning because of the fate of my friend Cesar.

Cesar was a flamboyant Spanish grandee who one autumn afternoon found some mushrooms in his girlfriend's yard and insisted they were delicious. She had her doubts, but he claimed they were savory, and she should add them to her salad. She said they look deadly, and he said, no, they will be delicious, and she said, no, don't eat them, and he said, even if they were poisonous, his love for her would conquer any toxins, and proceeded to consume one raw.

It turned out to be the destroying angel, *Amanita verna*, one of the deadliest of all mushrooms, and poor Cesar died a few days later.

I've been terrified of wild mushrooms ever since. But I eat them anyway.

Over the years I have seen various families of mushrooms appear and move on. For many seasons, in one section of the yard I used to find a host of mushrooms in the genus *Suillus*, around mid-September. *Suillus* are acid-loving and are commonly found in pine forests, and this happened to be in an area where I had, a few years earlier, taken out the last of the white pines from the original forest. Another year I had a good crop of oyster mushrooms growing on the stump of a Siberian elm that I had cut down. But a year later I dug out the stump and the oyster mushrooms went along with it. I also had a good crop of honey mushrooms for a while, but these too moved on for no apparent reason. (Actually, there was probably a very good reason, or reasons, but discovery of the disappearance would require intense analysis of weather patterns, soil conditions, spore distribution, and the age of the colony.)

I have also seen on old trees and stumps a number of turkey tail fungi, and also a few artist's fungi and other wood-dwelling species that I couldn't successfully identify. One of these, which I found in spring, growing on a false cypress, was one of the most repulsive-looking creatures I have ever discovered on the property. It resembled a bright orange, glistening octopus, except that it had multiple toxic-looking tentacles reaching out every which way, as if seeking a victim.

I am generally familiar with the different living things that occur in the garden even though I haven't accurately identified them. But this item I had never seen before, and I don't think it was one of those cases in which you don't see the obvious. This thing was genuinely disgusting. I photographed it and sent the image to my local mycologist, Dr. Lawrence Millman, who responded right away.

It turned out I had seen the species already, many times. Too many times, in fact. What I had discovered was the fruiting body of the cedar apple rust. This plant is a fungal pest on apples, and in some years it grows profusely on a border of Sargent crabs that are part of my teahouse allée. In late summer, I always would see the rusty brown spots growing on the leaves of the trees, and had identified them as rust. I knew from a college botany course that the spots were but one manifestation of a series of stages that the cedar apple rust goes through. It begins with small gray-brown galls that grow on the needles of native red cedar and other coniferous plants that I have in the garden. During wet weather, these relatively innocent-looking things absorb water, transform, and put out "horns," or telia, which produce the spores that infect the leaves of the apples with rusty brown spots. These form another fungal structure called aecia under the leaves, and these release more spores in dry weather that will infect the young leaves of the red cedar, which then goes on to produce the gall, which will then become the hideous octopus thing that I found. Interestingly, the fruiting body was growing on the needles of false cypress, and not my red cedars or arborvitae.

With the intention of expanding my limited fungi knowledge, and learning to see what I did not know, I invited the only slightly eccentric authority on mushroom matters, the aforementioned Lawrence Millman, to join me in a fungi foray in the middle of winter. He arrived with a small group of his mushroom-hunting companions and joined a group of interested friends of mine.

The day of the search turned out to be abnormal. It did not snow or sleet. There were no screaming northwest winds tearing at our cheeks. The temperature was nowhere near zero degrees Fahrenheit, the sun was actually shining, and in the strangest phenomenon of all, the grounds were clear of snow. There were five of us all told, and we began not twenty yards from the back porch, in a brushy area on the eastern boundary of the property.

Our leader was clad in high boots and sturdy trousers, a much-soiled cap, and carried with him in the form of a sidearm a magnifying loop and a mean-looking dagger for rooting around in soil and cutting off caps.

And so we intrepid explorers set out shortly after the winter sun fell below the crenellated towers of the guardian pines. We forged onward, past the terrace, down through a winter-killed garden patch, on through the tangles of brush and the ruins of a freakish, devastating Halloween snowstorm that had cascaded upon the garden while it was still in leaf, bringing down trees and branches, and in a single night accomplishing more than the usual damage of an entire winter.

Here we entered into a tangled brushy wood, whereupon, almost immediately, our leader discovered a species known as *Daedaleopsis confragosa*—or, in common parlance, the thin-walled maze polypore, a species common to Great Britain. Three minutes later Millman found a species of crust fungus growing on the underside of a log. He found a cheese polypore a few minutes later, then a collection of *Mycena* species, then a patch of lemon drops, and also a tinder polypore, a species that was among the possessions of Otzi, the Neolithic-era Ice Man whose five-thousand-year-old preserved body had turned up a few years earlier in a melting glacier. Onward then, as our leader discovered species after species of generally unseen and unknown fungi, as well as a slime mold known as wolf's milk, and a recent hatch of millipedes—in January, no less!

We moved slowly through the patch of land, progressing at no more than two or three yards in five minutes, while General Millman continued to hunt the underbellies of fallen limbs, mossy, dank spots, north-facing tree trunks, roots, and rotting logs, dead branches, and duff.

In the space of twenty minutes, in an area no more than ten by thirty or so yards, he found fifteen species all told, including those common enough to have garnered vernacular names, such as the tinder polypore, and lemon drops. He then flipped over a log, leaned over intently and inspected a white blob-like thing with his loop, and announced that this was possibly a new species of mushroom rarely found on this side of the Atlantic, and not entirely common in Europe, its native land. Somehow it had made its way to these shores. He said he would have to take it home to positively identify it.

The discovery of this many fungi in so small a plot of land got me thinking about the nature of the garden space. I wondered if Millman could find as many fungi in the depauperated white-pine forest on the other side of the western wall of the garden. Given the paucity of higher plants that I had found in the same pine forest on my side of the wall, I was certain that he couldn't. He said he could, and I said, I'll bet you, and he said, "Righto! A bottle of Laphroaig scotch, then."

And so we set out.

Within ten minutes he had found nearly five species. We ranged farther and farther away from the wall. He found three more. We pushed on north-northwest to one of the slopes that characterize the land on the western side of the drumlin. Three more. A little farther, and two others.

In the end, he did not find fifteen species. He found twenty-five, and I lost the bet. But Millman the Magnanimous invited me to share his prize a few days after I delivered the bottle to him.

This original survey gave me the idea to do it again, only this time in the height of the season of life, midsummer, and I decided to carry this out on a single day, in a sort of bio blitz, a variation of a local event that used to occur every July around the state, known as Biodiversity Day.

My day was a much smaller event, and consisted mostly of friends of mine who have knowledge of local plants and animals, some of them professional, some amateurs. The amateur status of the group was no slight on their ability to identify things in the field. One of the lengthy discussions that emerged from the professional botanists among the group was the tendency in our time of doing the most identification work inside sterile laboratories at the DNA level. Academically trained, younger biologists now spend less and less time out in the fields identifying the plants in their natural habitats. Some of the younger scientists are not even good field naturalists.

Not this group, though. Academics and amateurs alike were happy to get their feet wet, risk tick and mosquito bites, thorn-torn shirts, stings, and scratches.

Ideally they should have arrived before dawn to document the bird life. But I was already familiar with the larger, more obvious species of the grounds such the birds and mammals and the amphibians and reptiles. What I did not know, except in a casual sort of way, were the grasses, lichens, obscure fungi and herbaceous plants, insects, arachnids, worms, and other invertebrates that I knew were here—having seen them myself, but having had no idea what they were.

Our survey documented the fact that grasses, sedges, rushes, and reeds abound on the property, but inasmuch as this is generally acidic, poor soil, ferns are not so common. We located only six species. The same was true of lichens; very few in the actual garden, although if we ranged off the property down the path through Mr. Findlay's deciduous woods, there were many, four species on one rock alone, including the large leathery-leaved rock tripe, which is supposedly edible, if you are lost in the woods, that is, and starving. Flies and wasps and bees topped the insect list, and we located three species of worms, plus slugs, pill bugs, and millipedes, although these latter invertebrates were more common off the property in the deciduous forest. We had a harder time with spiders, but found a number of species within the various families of spiders including the orb weavers, jumping spiders, crab spiders in the flowers, funnel weavers, and grass spiders, house spiders, and a number of species of daddy longlegs, or harvestmen, of which there are more than seven thousand species worldwide. This had been a dry season, so mushrooms were few, and the liverworts, mosses, and other generally overlooked nonflowering plants were in recession. We did find a saprophyte, however, an Indian pipe that was just poking its curled pipe-head above the ground behind the Swan Cottage. Indian pipes and related species have no chlorophyll and attain their nutrients from decaying matter.

This was a hot day, and we had supplied cold beer, white wine, and an icy bowl of May wine, made with the sweet woodruff that abounds on the property. I am sorry to say that as the afternoon progressed, my survey team grew lax and one by one retired to the porch to cool themselves with a little liquid refreshment while reviewing the finds of the day. Plates of cheese arrived. A cold pasta à la primavera made with garden vegetables. More wine and beer. More stories from the local naturalists, more beer, and soon the sun sank below the pines, evening approached, and our supposed official survey petered out.

But the survey gave me an idea.

Every Fourth of July, for several years running, the American naturalist Edwin Way Teale would retire to a selected site on his land and sit in the same place all day, recording the plants and animals that happened along or grew there. Although I am hardly the naturalist that Teale was, I decided to do the same.

I picked an intimate, round garden room just in front of the teahouse on the south side of the garden. The place has good morning sun and by midday is shaded, so for a hot day in July it seemed a good choice, save for the fact that it is not the most botanically diverse section of the garden. The teahouse is covered with a climbing hydrangea on the right side, and a seabright honeysuckle on the left, a once popular but now rare nineteenth-century favorite that is hard to find.

The walls of the room itself consist of a "gateway" of boxwoods on the east and west, hollies and rhododendrons around the teahouse, lace-cap hydrangeas on either side of the gateway, and two beauty bushes framing the entrance to the room on the north. In spite of this lack of botanical diversity, I settled on one of the two benches in the room around seven in the morning with a thermos of coffee and a sketchbook and waited.

It would be more than tedious—unbearable, even—to list all the things that I saw, heard, smelled, and felt (in the form of insect bites) that day. But suffice to document here things seen between one o'clock and one thirty, which I calculated to be the quietest, least active time of the day, when the summer heat has laid most things low, including the local human population. The road and the distant highway were quiet, and the only sounds were the periodic whine of a passing housefly, the drumming of a red-bellied woodpecker on a dead tree by the western wall, and the distant crow of a rooster from the farm over the hill.

Insect life, by contrast, was active; I counted over twenty species in five or ten minutes, as well as four species of spider, plus the caterpillar of some unknown butterfly. Included in this group were the ever-present hoverflies, who seem to favor this site, especially in the morning when the sun begins to heat the room.

By sitting still, I noticed things that I passed every day and had not remarked upon: The Queen Anne's lace, about to bloom. The yarrow, blooming, along with the lace-cap hydrangeas and a blue hydrangea, and the berries setting on the inkberry and the hollies, and aphids on the stems of an errant Concord grape that was spreading itself over the hollies and hydrangeas, and a dragonfly snatching a gnat in midair, and a hole eaten in the screen of the teahouse by a mouse, and the old webs of some tiny spider, and the fact that my epimediums were spreading all across the teahouse steps and needed cutting back, and that a yellow lily I had forgotten about was in bloom, and that the beauty bush had gone to seed. All this and more.

I should also confess that I grew hungry and went in the house for lunch at one point, and came back and retreated to the couch in the teahouse for a nap around two thirty, and then, oppressed by the heat, I took a break and went for a swim at the local lake. I came back to watch things, and then later, as evening settled in, enjoyed a few glasses of cold prosecco with a gardening friend.

As night fell a pale green suffused the sky and my friend and I surveyed the upper airs for bats. One bat appeared, a species known as the big brown bat, judging from the size. But I am sorry to say, the arrival of this single species was a sad comment on the state of bats in the Northeast.

For years, one of the early-evening entertainments for the children of the garden was bat watching and attempted bat catching. The air in those times was filled with little brown bats, pipistrelles, and big browns, flitting and diving all across the clearing above the garden. We would collect pebbles and throw one into the sky at a bat and watch it spiral down after the falling pebble, checking it out to see whether it was some large, edible insect.

Now the green evening sky is empty of bats. A hideous fungal ailment known as white-nose syndrome has seriously affected the entire eastern populations of the most common bat in the region, the handsome little brown bat.

These bats hibernate clustered together in caves and mines, and although not much is known about white-nose syndrome, it is theorized that the bats pass the disease from one to another as they shuffle around during their winter sleep. The fungus also occurs among European bats, but they seem to have adjusted to the illness over the eons and are not seriously affected. Somehow, the fungus made it to North America a few years ago, and now it is spreading. About 90 percent of the eastern population of little brown bats has been wiped out, and the disease has affected colonies of other species that hibernate clustered together. Species such as the red bat that nest in trees do not get infected, nor do species that hibernate singly or in houses and barns, such as the big brown bat.

We waited quietly in front of the teahouse until the green sky darkened to a deeper shade, while the feeding bat continued its lonely aerial acrobatics. In the distance we could hear the deep-throated rumble of July Fourth fireworks blasting off from a nearby town, and then, from the brushy edges of the hydrangeas, I heard the singular summer call of a meadow cricket.

Such were the observations of a single day in July and the two worlds that exist side by side on this planet, the world of we late-arriving Cro-Magnons, and the more ancient wild world of our nonhuman fellow travelers.

6.

Frog Pond

Old frog pond
Frog jumps in
Water sound

✳ Basho

American colonial gardens often maintained small plots known as the wilderness, based on the Italian traditional *bosco* in which the original, uncultivated vegetation of the place was allowed to flourish. I maintained such a plot on the northwest side of the property that contains, along with a line of red maples, a vernal pool where frogs and salamanders breed.

From March to June this area is covered with standing water, but late in the spring the whole floor flourishes with bellwort, mayflower, whorled loosestrife, swamp candles, and fine stands of royal fern, sensitive fern, wood ferns, and interrupted ferns.

This particular vernal pool is the breeding area of the wood frogs and toads that I see around the garden later in the season, as well as the occasional yellow-spotted and blue-spotted salamanders I come across. Since I have left the nearby dead trees standing, the woodlot is also a haven for woodpeckers and the various species of wood-boring insects upon which the woodpeckers feed. Mallard ducks occasionally settle in this small wetland in spring,

and every year wood ducks raise a family in a tree hollow just beyond the garden wall.

I am of the opinion that a sign of a good, healthy garden is
the presence of toads and frogs. Toads especially are avid consumers of garden pests such as cutworms, slugs, Japanese beetle grubs,
cucumber beetles, millipedes, earwigs, grasshoppers, and anything
else that resides in a cultivated garden plot, including, I am sorry
to report, some beneficial creatures, such as earthworms and spiders. They are ravenous eaters. It has been estimated that a single
toad can eat as many as fifty to one hundred insects and other invertebrates in a single night, which is about three times more than
its own weight. This calculates to something like ten thousand or
more pests in the course of a growing season, of which at least 80
percent are pest species.

Mrs. Theodosia Huntingfield, it turns out, is quite fond of
toads herself and maintains a toad sanctuary at her gardens in
Royal Tunbridge Wells. Her property, which I have visited on several occasions, is located in a section of the village in which the
houses in her area surround a common, consisting of a wildwood.
This is a watery, low area with a pond and, in spring, a rivulet or
two, and is fine habitat for toads. From this common ground, they
stray into her garden and are warmly welcomed. All about her
property she has set small, artificial walls with many nooks and
crannies, as well as her versions of what she calls her Toad Halls.
(As you might imagine, Mrs. Huntingfield esteems the creatures
of *The Wind in the Willows.*)

Her "halls" are tiles or slates laid across two bricks about loose,
cultivated soil, fit for burrowing. Toads prefer a moist, cool envi-

ronment and are good diggers. They will back into their halls, excavating with their hind legs, and spend the heat of the day — such as it is in Olde England — sheltering from the sun. They emerge at dusk and feed at night.

I have installed similar toad sanctuaries in the Vicarage Garden but these consist of broken clay flowerpots, which I set out in the various cultivated plots around the gardens. I'm certain that toads use them, but I rarely see them in their houses; they always seem to be out foraging, even in the daytime. Ironically, one of their favorite hangouts is a small flagstone path and terrace just off the back porch. This section gets the full blast of summer afternoon sun and is an unlikely habitat for damp-loving creatures such as toads. And yet after dark I often see them in this area, I think partly because insects collect there, attracted by the lights on the back porch, which serves as a combination living room, dining room all summer long. The toads shelter during the day in the dank soil just under the kitchen widow, near a hose spigot and its surround of Manhattan euonymus and boxwood, which shades that part of the house. The toads have the best of both worlds there, cool moist soil in the day and an abundance of insects by night.

Perhaps because of this habitat I often find toads and frogs on the porch itself. I think they must come in through holes in our ill-maintained screens, or through a homemade dog door, consisting of a screen flap with a weight at the bottom. The toads and green frogs that arrive, I always catch and release. But, since they are great consumers of insects such as mosquitoes, I am inclined to leave the tree frogs that also make it in. We sometimes see them clinging to the insides of the screens, as well as the outside. These are generally spring peepers, which seem to range everywhere in the garden, but occasionally I find the larger and more colorful gray tree frogs.

One summer night I found a small bright emerald-green frog on the screen—a new species for New England, I thought, and hoped! I waded through my various guides to reptiles and amphibians in an attempt to identify the tiny frog and learned that, when they are young, the gray tree frogs are smaller and bright green. This one I set free immediately, since I am trying to encourage the presence of gray tree frogs on this property. I love to hear their bird-like, sultry chirping on hot summer evenings before rain. They sing of ancient evenings and the warm South.

They also say something about the ability of cold-blooded creatures such as reptiles and amphibians to survive northern winters. In the case of the gray tree frog, and also the wood frog, this strategy takes on a rather extreme form. They actually freeze thoroughly in winter.

Both species hibernate just below the leaf level, or under loose bark in the case of the gray tree frog. Neither of these shelters provides much protection, and as soon as the temperature begins to drop below freezing, ice crystals begin to form in the outer layers of their skin. In the meantime, this action seems to cause the frogs to release glucose, which will saturate their organs. Basically, the sugars form a syrupy mix inside their cells, whereas the outside is by then surrounded by ice crystals. Eventually, as the frost progresses, the entire frog will freeze solid. They stop breathing; their hearts no longer beat, and they will remain in this zombie-like condition until the spring thaws arrive. It seems miraculous, but both wood frogs and gray tree frogs range as far north as northern Canada, and have survived in these regions ever since the glaciers retreated.

Most turtles survive the winter by burrowing down in the muddy bottoms of ponds and remaining through the season in a sort of suspended animation. But a few, such as the young of the painted turtle and the snapping turtle, use the same strategy that the wood frogs and tree frogs use. They remain in their nests near where they were hatched and just allow themselves to freeze. Then in late spring they unfreeze, wake up, and begin wandering.

In late spring you see baby painted turtles and snappers all over the two roads that cut through Scratch Flat. Unfortunately, many of them get squashed by passing cars as they emerge from the marshes of the brook and attempt to move to new territory. Wandering adults often meet the same fate. I counted five dead turtles in the space of a few yards one summer day, including the increasingly rare spotted turtle.

Fortunately, the state wildlife authorities, responding to out-cries from turtle lovers, constructed turtle-exclusion barriers on either side of a bridge on the busiest road, and turtle mortality on that road at least has been reduced.

Early one hot summer morning I rescued a box turtle that was thinking to cross one of these roads. It was halfway over, and was staring back at a car that had fortunately swerved to miss it. Naturally, passing cars notwithstanding, I pulled over.

Box turtles, along with the spotted turtle and the Blanding's turtle, are now rare in this part of the world, having fallen victim to new housing developments and roads of this sort.

Stopping to rescue turtles is a habit I have had for years now. I have swung onto the rough narrow verges of innumerable back roads and highways to wave away cars from painted turtles, box turtles, and baby turtles of all common species, as well as those huge tanks of female snappers that appear on suburban roads, headed for the sandy banks where they go to lay their eggs in the month of June. It's probably an unsafe habit—standing there by the side of a road while the indifferent commuters wheel by at illegal rates of speed. But what choice is there? In some ways I look at turtle rescue as an existential act. By saving one, you promote salvation for all turtles.

This particular box turtle was in a quandary. To the east lay an interstate highway. To the south there was a busy state road, thick with traffic. West lay a barrier of mini mansions with driveways and manicured lawns, and to the north lay the busy road that crosses the brook. The turtle was, with no pun intended, boxed in, a condition in which much of our contemporary wildlife finds itself.

Box turtles used to be common in the dry uplands around these parts. They favor light, open woods, and wet meadows, and can often be found near, although not necessarily in, streams and ponds. They'll eat almost anything, even carrion, but appear to love strawberries and blackberries, flowers, roots, and other vegetation, and also slugs, worms, frogs, salamanders, and almost any other edible living or dead thing they can manage to swallow. They appear to be homebodies, never traveling very far within the circumscribed lives of their home territories, which may be no larger than two or three hundred yards. They hibernate in winter, are abroad all summer and into the fall, and they mate in spring and summer. The females lay several clutches of eggs in a sandy bank or loose soil. The young hatch out in about three months, depending on the ambient temperature.

The box turtles' most famous trick is that they can shut themselves up entirely inside their hinged shell if they think they're in danger. They'll wait in this position until they perceive that their enemies have moved on. Because of this survival technique they actually do not have very many enemies, save for one, a major one—the bulldozer.

Development pressure, highway construction, shopping malls and housing, and to some extent the pet trade, and the mere presence of roads, have driven the box turtle to the edge of extirpation in some areas. It is under siege throughout its range, which includes most of eastern North America.

I caught this particular box turtle and brought her up to my aspen grove and examined her. (I could tell she was a female by her long slender hind claws and yellowish eyes.) My inclination was to put her inside the fenced greens garden and let her live there for the summer. Gilbert White had a pet turtle of this sort named Timothy that he kept in his garden in Selborne, and I thought that I could do the same with this turtle. I could keep her inside my various garden rooms and let her feed at will.

With this in mind, I put her in the semi-shaded garden where I grow greens, pulled up a chair that I keep in the birch grove over by the edge of the garden, and watched to see what she would do.

After a few minutes, having decided that all danger had passed, she poked her head out and looked around, dully. Then she lumbered northward at a diagonal through the garden and stopped, once more staring at her new surroundings. Then she changed course, moved on a little farther, and stopped again. This went on for twenty minutes or so until, as if understanding, finally, that she had arrived in some turtlesque Eden of sorts, she snatched a bite from a large kale leaf. Satisfied that she had become comfortable in her new environment, I carried on with my own ramblings through my own Eden and more or less forgot about her. Late in the afternoon I went back and discovered that she was still there, and had helped herself to more kale and collards. This caused me to undertake some reflection. This was July, and if I let her stay in this garden for the rest of the summer, she would likely finish off all my carefully tended plantings. I had purposely fenced this garden to keep turkeys and rabbits from this section of the property and if I let Cynthia (her name, I presumed—she looked like a Cynthia) have her way, she would surely do more damage than a whole flock of turkeys. So I decided to let her go.

I set her free on the wild side of the garden wall where the woodland slopes down to a low valley that runs up to the southern side of a small lake. South of the woodlands there are two working farms, rich with lettuce and other delicacies. The nearest road is nearly a quarter mile away to the southwest. Given the fact that a box turtle's range is measured in yards, I carried her down into the hollow, placed her carefully among some delicious wild strawberries, and wished her Godspeed. She remained closed up in her new land for a few minutes and then slowly emerged and, without surveying the territory, lumbered off into the brush as if she knew exactly where she was headed in life.

Turtles do not commonly occur in my Scratch Flat garden, save for the ones I bring home, hoping to introduce to my side of Eden. Frogs, by contrast, come on their own, partly because I have purposely created a habitat here to encourage them. Actually, it does not take much work to bring in frogs and toads. The best thing you can do is nothing.

The house on the eastern side of the compound where I first lived was once a paradise of frogs. There was a fallen barn and an old uncut lawn in back of the house and a few apple trees, backed by the deep woods, complete with vernal pools where the new Vicarage Garden is now located. The yard, such as it was, was characterized mainly by amphibians. Wherever you walked it seemed that something was hopping out of your way, either a toad, or a wood frog, or later in the summer, a pickerel frog. I would keep the grasses down with a scythe on that property, and sleek-bodied pickerel frogs would execute fantastic crisscrossing leaps to escape with every third or fourth swing. I once found a gray tree frog in a hole in one of the old apple trees while I was out scything, and sometimes, after long rainy spells in spring, we would find frogs in the house, wood frogs in the cellar, along with salamanders, spring peepers in the kitchen, and once, a gray tree frog on the dining room window.

Slowly, in the course of gentrification of the grounds, I began mowing the lawn and digging in flower beds and cleaning up the fallen barn and the assorted detritus that had collected there ever since the old farmer who once owned this place went to his reward. The constant annual scything of the grasses under the apple trees, finally, as I had hoped, evicted the poison ivy and the multiflora rose and the blackberry. But the pickerel frogs also departed. Toads no longer lingered around the porch lights, and I rarely saw any frogs on my lawn. What's worse, development began creeping into the former fields and woods around the house, and sadly, year by year, the spring peeper chorus diminished, and I heard less and less the beautiful birdlike trilling of the gray tree frogs.

I determined after that experience to attempt to turn the Vicarage Garden into as much of a frog sanctuary as I could without turning the whole property over to an artificial pond surrounded by wetlands. So I began digging out, deepening, and slowing down the running water of the intermittent stream that runs down along the north wall of the grounds each spring.

In the time of the pine forest, this tract of land had no frogs whatsoever as far as I could tell. But the series of vernal pools on the northern side of the property where the woods were deciduous was good breeding territory. I thought I could help the vernal-pool dwellers if they also had a few deeper pools to visit in summer, after the vernal pools dried out. With this in mind, just below the vernal pools and near the intermittent stream, I tried to create a frog pond.

The first was just a shallow, scooped-out area that I lined with concrete. I dug a shallow hole, poured in concrete, and let it set. I filled it on a rainy day in early April, and the very next morning I looked out from the back porch and saw a toad sitting on a rock I had placed in a shallow end. Quick work, I thought.

Unfortunately, within a week, through some process of osmosis, the frog pond began to drain itself. I filled it again and it leaked out once more. I bought sealer and painted the bottom to no avail, and in the end I had to go out and buy one of those black pool liners. To disguise its inherent ugliness, I gave this liner a skim coat of cement, and then filled it again. A month later, as summer approached, no less than three green frogs moved in.

Inspired by this, I dug out another small pond farther from the house and put in another premade fish pond someone had given me. Within a few days more green frogs took up residence, and at the end of summer, a bullfrog settled in. He must have wintered in the marshes around the brook. But he came back in the late spring and spent the next summer there.

Finally, I put in another ornamental pond just outside the back terrace and fitted it with a fountain and stocked it with a couple of goldfish. This pool was nestled in between two boxwood hedges and a brace of pleached pear trees, and it became the most attractive pool on the property as far as the frogs were concerned. The bullfrog deserted his original pond and moved to the fountain pool and stayed there for two or three summers. He had such a regular presence, he was given a name. For whatever possible reason I do not know, one of the children named him William. He was so tame you could stroke his nose if you approached him slowly, and he became a welcome attraction to visiting children, some of whom, I believe, had never seen a real frog, let alone stroked one's nose.

In the meantime, I planted more sheltered flower beds, and allowed the grasses to grow tall and weedy on my version of a lawn, and created shrub borders to grow along the back walls. As a result, the frog population began to increase. I then built several little toolsheds, which were intended not necessarily for tools but to serve as hiding places for mice and snakes, eaves for nesting birds, and a sanctuary for toads, who used to hide underneath the sheds in the heat of the day.

Along with so many good things, frogs too are in decline worldwide and no one knows quite why. The probable causes are legion: habitat destruction, global climate change, and, in the tropics, where the decline is most dramatic, a fungal pathogen that has devastating effects on most species wherever it moves into new regions.

Given this depressing scenario, perhaps the most satisfying thing one can do is go out and dig frog ponds.

7.

The Labyrinth

The sedge is wither'd from the lake,
And no birds sing.

✳ JOHN KEATS

I grew up in a town famous for its old trees and gardens and also for its birdlife. Among other things, the Christmas Bird Count was started in the town in 1900 by the ornithologist Frank Chapman and a few of his bird-watching cronies. There was a landscaped hillside across from my bedroom window, and one of my earliest memories is of the vast rolling chorus of robins, doves, thrushes, and unidentifiable (at least to me) squeaks, whistles, chirps, buzzings, and peeps that would pour in my window on spring mornings like a waterfall. I never thought about this polyphonic bird chorus; it was just there, part of my world.

My family had come north from the Eastern Shore of Maryland, and on summer visits to the rural settings of the old family farms and town gardens, the dawn chorus of birds was equally loud, as was the daylong, winsome call of the bobwhites, and also the calls of the huge barking flocks of crows that would dip and roll across the cornfields. At night on my cousin's river farm, I lay awake listening to the dark *quock* of night herons sounding out from the riverbanks, and by day we lived with the eternal cries of circling ospreys, and the air filled with darting swallows. I even used to see bald eagles there, a rare event back then.

After that I lived in deep woods, in northwestern Connecticut, where there were vast migrations of wood warblers each spring and then again in the fall. That was also owl country; the odd caterwauls of barred owls rang out from the nearby swampy lowlands in autumn and again in spring. I would hear the ghostly whinny of the screech owl all through the summer, and the deep booming of the great horned owl on late winter nights, along with other unidentifiable shrieks and calls, probably long-eared owls. Also on summer nights there I used to be awakened by the mysterious night song of the ovenbird.

When I first moved to Scratch Flat, the scrubby pasture just north of the house was loud with the calls of prairie warblers and blue-winged warblers in spring. All along the brushy edges of the property the yellow warblers and yellowthroats nested. The indigo buntings would be singing madly by June, and every day the woodland edges were pierced with the sharp call of the great crested flycatcher. I used to see kingbirds in a nearby orchard; the woods to the west, just beyond the garden wall, were alive with the songs of veeries, wood thrushes, ovenbirds, and black and white warblers, as well as ruby-crowned kinglets and parula warblers. And east of the house, where the hayfields dropped down to the marshes of the brook, barn swallows and tree swallows coursed the fields from dawn to dusk. Hooded mergansers, marsh wrens, green herons, and even the occasional bittern and sora rail used to appear in the marshes from time to time, and wood ducks still nested in hollow trees around the vernal pools on Mr. Findlay's wooded grounds.

These latter were the source, incidentally, of a dragon I once spotted in the garden.

I was sitting in the kitchen with a child on my lap when I looked out the window and saw a snake-like animal with a long neck—a raised reptilian head, and a long undulating body with what appeared to be scales on its back. I myself was fooled for a second or two, but soon realized it was a mother wood duck passing through the hickory grove with ten ducklings in a row behind her. I grabbed the child and we fled outdoors to see if we could get a better look, but by that time she was gone.

More recently, on a June morning in the year of the wedding, I heard the song of a black-billed cuckoo. That got me thinking about local birds. How long ago had it been since I last heard a black-billed cuckoo in the yard? For that matter, how long had it been since I had heard the plaintive dawn song of the wood pewee? Or the night wailing of the whip-poor-will? That year, other than the black-billed cuckoo, and one ovenbird, plus the usual array of garden birds such as blue jays and song sparrows, the spring was silent. The same phenomenon was taking place all through the town and beyond. The woods and fields have gone to development, and no birds sing.

Academic ornithologists might suggest that this is mere anecdotal evidence and one would need more objective and broader field analysis of data to determine that there is truly a decline in bird populations. But this sort of anecdotal evidence is a story you hear over and over again. And in reality, now the facts of a massive worldwide descent are everywhere in scientific papers. It appears that the whole class of Aves, a group that evolved from dinosaurs some 160 million years ago, for a variety of reasons, is coming to an end.

But while there does appear to be a general decline, the situation is slightly more complex. In fact, some species of birds are increasing around my Scratch Flat garden and elsewhere in the region.

Part of the loss of diversity of local birds around the Vicarage Garden is perhaps not so much a case of overuse of pesticides. In spite of the fact that Scratch Flat was an actively farmed tract of land up until the 1970s, with free use—I assume—of toxic chlorinated hydrocarbons such as DDT and chlordane, bird populations were seemingly healthy when I first moved here. What has altered dramatically is the change in habitat. And what has happened here is the same thing that is happening all over the Northeast. Quite apart from the loss of habitat, the land is returning to the biological community that existed here in 1620, when the Pilgrims first settled.

One of the best descriptions of this North American environment, in my view, comes from William Bradford's *Of Plimouth Plantation*. He recounts what the Pilgrims witnessed—and felt—when they first viewed the November landscape of southeastern Massachusetts: "What could they see but a hideous and desolate wilderness full of wild beasts and wild men ... and the whole country full of woods and thickets represented a wild and savage hue."

In that desolate wilderness, there were no blue-winged or prairie warblers. Meadowlarks did not call, nor would the Pilgrims have heard the sharp whistle of the cowbird or the trill of field sparrows. All these species are midwestern birds of the open lands. They would have appeared in this region only after the forests were cleared by the descendants of Bradford's Pilgrims and those who followed. The often-cited statistic holds that in the 1850s, 85 percent of the Northeast was cleared, and 15 percent was forest or dense urban areas. Now the statistic is reversed and the region is mostly forest. But the makeup of that forest has altered.

With the exception of the American chestnut, tree species such as oak, maple, beech, and hickory and ash may be the same as the first settlers faced, but there are no longer any vast areas of dense forest. Except for large expanses of unbroken spruce fir forests in the far North, most of the woods have houses and small developments nestled in among the trees. As a result, the extensive forest cover is broken up by yards and roads and parking lots, and there is a decline in birds that nest in the deep forest. Species such as the wood thrush, veery, and red-eyed vireo need large areas of unbroken woodland in order to nest successfully. Species of this sort prefer nesting areas that are at least two or three hundred yards from open spaces such as my garden.

In the face of this, however, there are certain groups of birds in the Northeast whose populations are actually increasing. For one thing, partly because of warming climate conditions, and partly because of the popularity of winter bird-feeding, many southern species are drifting northward. Here on Scratch Flat in the early 1960s you would rarely, if ever, see a Carolina wren, or a titmouse, or cardinal, turkey, red-bellied woodpecker, or mockingbird. All these species are now common around the Vicarage Garden. Also spreading northward are many species I do not see around Scratch

Flat but which have moved into the general area. These include turkey vultures, blue-gray gnatcatchers, hooded warblers, and the blue-winged warbler.

Furthermore, some birds seem to me to be indestructible, not necessarily because of their ability to adapt to changing environments, but mainly because of their character, or personality, if one could say such a thing about a species of bird. Among these, in my unscientific opinion, is the house wren.

On any given morning between May 5th and May 10th, I can step out into the garden and hear, for the first time in five months, the incessant, even frenetic, trilling of house wrens. They come in with the south wind, usually on a clear sunny morning, and go out with far less flourish, on the northwest wind five months later.

The male is the first to arrive, and he goes around "his" land (not mine!) stating his presence in no uncertain terms. He's been here before, and he knows his way around.

The female appears a few days later. And after a certain amount of ritual and restatements of territorial boundaries by the male—none of which I can follow—the two of them will begin work on a nest in a palatial birdhouse I have set up in back of the garden. They spend the spring and early summer there, flitting around, getting angry, chattering madly, and hunting through the shrubbery for spiders and caterpillars.

Bird aficionados are not supposed to like wrens. They're noisy little devils, for one thing, and they have some very nasty habits. Once they've crammed their bulky stick nests into whatever convenient crevice they can find, they'll range around their property pecking the eggs of other nesting birds, almost out of spite, it would seem. Furthermore, they are not—how shall I say—the most beautiful bird in the backyard. They are patterned with a few dark stripes against a dull wood-colored brown background, a whitish belly, and they have a mean little decurved bill that looks like it was designed for surgical purposes. Nor are they loyal mates. Once they have set up housekeeping and the female is incubating the eggs, the male patrols his territory seeking other females.

Given all this, they have not endeared themselves to those who seek wholesome metaphors about family life from the world of birds—even their semi-musical trilling becomes tedious when you hear it every minute or so throughout the daylight hours.

In spite of all this, I am partial to wrens. I like their spunk. I like their cocky little tails and beady eyes, and the way they get mad at anything in their path and begin whispering and chattering at cats and dogs and even people.

For several years running, a pair utilized a little wren house I fitted onto one of the posts in a grape arbor I planted along the trellis allée that leads back to the woods on the southwest side of the property. On my way to the greens garden on the southeast side of the allée I am inevitably assailed as I pass their house. One of the pair will follow me along the grape wall, chipping and chattering, and flitting its wings angrily as if this tiny sprite had the ability to drive off the annoying, slow-moving primate that has the audacity to come near its yard.

But mostly what I like about wrens is their predestined willingness to undertake marathon flights from the cold gardens of New England and Canada, south to Florida, and even beyond, into Central and South America. It seems somehow unfathomable that these tiny packages can summon the energy to fly all the way down the length of a continent and back up again in the course of one year, select mates, and then go about the business of raising children, only to turn around and go back south again in autumn.

Sometime in the summer, I don't know when exactly, since they slip out quietly, the wrens leave my garden. They fade from the sunny borders and move back into the shady woods, where they spend the late summer and early autumn feeding low to the ground, no longer singing, and assuming a certain hardworking, businesslike affect. I see them out there from time to time in the woodlot and the Bishop's Close, dark and low and fast moving, like quick mice.

Perhaps they need to lay low in this manner in late summer. They have a long trip ahead of them.

Although a few individuals may hang around the northern woods until November, most house wrens begin their mass exodus in September. Like many land birds, they move south in fits and starts, and like most migrants, they run into hardships all along the way. Storms carry them far out to sea. Headwinds batter them, cats eat them, and along with a growing number of land birds nowadays, wrens crash into things at night. Fifty years ago these obstacles were radio towers, water towers, and city skyscrapers. Now, as do all migratory land birds, wrens have to contend with the proliferation of cell phone towers and windmills.

Wrens are not long-distance migrants in the manner of swifts or nighthawks, or even warblers and hummingbirds. They generally only go as far south as Florida. But it is this lack of limelight, that businesslike, dogged manner, that I like about them. They're working birds, energetic little sparks of life in a hard rock world.

I daresay they will be among the last bird to become extinct.

❊❊❊❊❊

Of all the garden spaces on these grounds, one of the most densely populated with different bird species is the maze. The labyrinth (the terms are interchangeable in older dictionaries) consists of eleven courses, or paths, and after a few years it became a habitat in itself, where cardinals and sparrows would nest each season, ground covers spread on their own, and children and other wild creatures would dart and weave to and fro on summer afternoons. For the hedge material I used Siberian elm, which I selected because it is a fast-growing, hardy tree—or hedge, if you keep it clipped. What I did not realize is the fact that it is difficult to hold at bay. I have to clip it regularly, and as new beds and new projects began to accumulate, especially during the year of the wedding, I had less and less time to keep it trimmed. At one point it got so high I could no longer reach the top, even with long-handled hedge clippers. In the end, I had to resort to the use of a power hedge clipper at the end of a long pole.

Maintenance of the labyrinth may have been a chore for me, but the spiders, snakes, meadow mice, turkeys, crickets, and various birds did not mind a little disorder. One year, three different species of birds nested in that one tangled network of branches. And another year I found, after the leaves were off the hedge walls, that three different species of hornets and yellow jackets had nested there. We walked by them all summer long without so much as a single sting.

For a while, I had a bird feeder in the goal, as the center of a maze is called, so that blue jays and redwings and other feeders would form a funnel-like flock over the center. I also attempted to train the Jack Russell to run the maze by throwing a tennis ball from the entrance into the goal, hoping he would run the eleven courses to get to the center to retrieve the ball. He soon learned to burrow through the hedge walls, though, so I gave up on the sport.

There were many other species of birds nesting elsewhere in the garden: wrens in wren boxes, starlings, and English sparrows in house crevices, a phoebe over the kitchen door, song sparrows in the Fraser fir along the trellis allée, woodpeckers in the dead trees I left standing, mourning doves, robins, of course, and, in the earlier years, yellow warblers, yellowthroats, great crested flycatchers, and, until the barn across the street was torn down, barn swallows, tree swallows, and bluebirds that nested in boxes I put up later, after the old fields were cleared on the tangle of invasive shrubs.

Along with the catbirds, robins, wrens, hummingbirds, et al., another local nester in the Vicarage Garden was the seemingly ever-present Baltimore oriole, a species that is often seen and heard but which has been declining over the past three or four decades. A handsome couple of orioles nested in a willow tree in the garden for several years.

The English Lady, who was not familiar with the species, used to refer to them as the Duke and Duchess. After all, as she pointed out, he dresses in a red orange waistcoat, a black cap that covers most of his head, and a velvety black jacket decorated with white patches, and she, the more modest of the two, always wears a subtle bodice of pale green, with a dark cape. Lady Theodosia, who met them one May afternoon, said they reminded her of the Duke and Duchess of Windsor inasmuch as she, the so-called Duchess, was theoretically from Baltimore, Maryland, where Mrs. Wallis Simpson, the American-born wife of the real duke, was from. More accurately, I believe, she should have named them (if you must name them at all) the Duke and Duchess of Malpais, after a small, somewhat run-down village on the Pacific coast of Costa Rica, where they might have lived.

They were hardly nobility, of course, they were merely birds, albeit handsome birds. Their real names, or at least the name given to the species in Costa Rica, is *bolsero norteño*, which translates to something fundamentally mundane, like "northern sack maker." Costa Ricans also call them, unofficially, *cabezas negras*, "black heads," but that is probably a local name given to the birds by the people who live among them day to day. In the scientific community, north, south, and the world around, they are called *Icterus galbula* (in Latin, not Spanish) and they belong, generally, to the family of blackbirds, as do all orioles.

Basically, Baltimore orioles are tropical birds, as are many of the bird families that nest in this garden. Over eons of evolution, these various tropical species have developed the habit of coming up to North America to breed. Or as some theories hold, they were originally northern species, driven to the tropics by glaciers, that came back after the ice disappeared as a result of some deep, atavistic habit.

In either case, the fact is, they are not "our" birds, as so many garden and field guides and popular essays state. They are Costa Ricans, or Nicaraguans, or nationals of any of the many little countries of Central and South America. They come up here for the same reason many of the human citizens of the northern United States go south in winter on vacations—to mate. The difference is that the orioles have children while they're on vacation, and stick around to feed and house them. Then they go back home.

One winter, when the garden had transformed itself into a white palace of turrets and ice walls, and the white towers of some mystic Snow Queen, I deserted Scratch Flat and followed "my" orioles south to the town of Malpais, on the Nicoya Peninsula, in Costa Rica. I wanted to see how the Duke and his Duchess were faring in their homeland.

It turns out that so far—in the region around Malpais, at least, unlike other parts of Central America, which are losing bird habitats at an alarming rate—the orioles are doing quite well.

Up until the 1950s, this section of Costa Rica was covered with dry tropical forest, not the deep rainforest that you find to the south on the Osa Peninsula, nor the dry scrub of the northern part of the Nicoya. But American foresters set up timber companies in the region and soon cleared most of the trees. The area had been sparsely populated when it was forested, but once the trees were cleared, settlers moved in and began raising cattle. By the late twentieth century, cattle ranching was in decline, and a new economy arrived in the form of tourism. This latest development was led, not by big spenders who pay a lot of money to stay in well-appointed resorts and sleep all day by elaborate swimming pools or play golf. This section of the country was characterized by smaller ecolodges, encouraged, ironically, by a coterie of international surfers who would come here from as far away as Israel. This coast happens to have some of the heaviest surf in the world and wide shoaling beaches.

Following on the heels of the surfers came another benign species of visitor, the ecotourist. Neither the surfers, who were content to camp on the beach by night and surf by day, nor the ecotourists were particularly interested in seeing the region further despoiled; quite the opposite, in fact. And this latest change in the local economy has been good for orioles.

The Baltimore oriole is a species that could get along quite well with the effects of human development and alteration of habitat—to a degree. A few decades back, persistent pesticides could have been the undoing of this handsome bird—along with many others. Sections of Cambridge, Massachusetts, for example, which were heavily sprayed in the 1950s and '60s, still do not have nesting orioles, whereas nearby sections in Massachusetts, where spraying was limited, do. There are still pressures on orioles in North America, such as increased habitat destruction and, most recently, the omnipresence of cell towers and radio towers, which have the effect of killing migratory birds that hit them at night during migration. The loss of the elm, a favorite nesting tree, has also played a part in the decline. But the versatile oriole has found other trees—such as my willows. The edge habitat that orioles seem to favor has been increasing, pesticide use is theoretically regulated in the North, and, if some far-thinking agencies would do something to halt the spread or even cut back on the profusion of towers, the future for the oriole at the northern end of its range could be assured.

My Baltimore orioles show up in the yard sometime around the beginning of May. And the Duke, as befitting dukes the world around, enters his property in grand style. He announces himself by flying from treetop to treetop, calling out his—to some ears—tedious song over and over again, the herald of spring. Baltimore orioles invariably arrive when the apples blossom, and the scented air, coupled with the repetitive whistled voluntaries, animates all outdoors. A dramatic entrance indeed.

Their real story begins in Central America in late February, when the sun rises slightly earlier than it does in mid-winter, and sets later. This subtle change in light is enough to rekindle in the pair a renewed interest in one another (or for that matter in any available Baltimore oriole of the opposite sex). Both males and females exhibit what the Germans call *Zugunruhe*, a certain premigratory restlessness. The males begin to sing at this time as if in practice for the big performance, which comes later in May.

In late February, *Zugunruhe* gets the better of the orioles, and they begin for the North, flying by night, resting and feeding by day, and moving north with the spring at an average rate of roughly twelve miles a day. By April, depending on the weather conditions, those who have wintered along the west coast of Central America will begin arriving on the Gulf coasts of the United States. By mid-April they can be seen in the Mid-Atlantic states, and by early May the vanguard of males will arrive in the North. Other males begin to pour in, and then the females show up about a week later after the first males arrive.

During the four years that the orioles lived in my willow trees, the Duke would make his appearance around the 2nd or 3rd of May, and he would arrive always at dawn. One day he would not be there and then the next morning, there he was, announcing himself with his characteristic two-note theme and variation. I would always hear him before I would see him, sometimes before I was even out of bed. I'd rise up, get out to the garden, and there would be the Duke himself, in the tops of the surrounding trees, poking around the leaves, plucking off insects as if he had been there all year.

The Duchess would usually arrive a few days later, and once she was in town there would follow a great deal of singing and courtship. The Duke would go about the yard singing and chattering and hopping from branch to branch, and in his finest hours, bowing formally to his lady in a stately pavane, lowering his wings and fanning out his tail feathers to reveal the finery of his attire.

From time to time he was forced to fend off intruders who dared to breach the invisible (to us, at least) walls of his sacrosanct territory. These included other male oriole suitors of the Duchess, as well as one of my cats, who would perchance saunter by with complete indifference, but would evoke nonetheless much chattering and screeching and not a few dive-bombing runs, which would also arouse the resident blue jays and a local mockingbird. Sometimes acting in concert, these three species would manage to drive the cat home to his couch on the back porch.

At some point during this courtship period, someplace discreetly out of sight, these handsome birds would mate. Even before mating, however, within a week or two of their arrival the Duchess would have selected a site for the nest. In my garden, the site was always the same, the drooping end of a weeping willow tree above the toolshed I had salvaged. The Duchess herself would do all the work, although the Duke would come by and perform periodic inspections, and would even get into the nest before it was completed, as if to test its suitability. This nest building among orioles and oropendolas—the sack-nesting genus of birds—approaches the level of art. It requires an elaborate weaving process with nest material poked inward, and then drawn outward, and then woven together in such a way as to withstand high winds and rain.

Some weeks after mating, the Duchess would lay four eggs in her nest and begin brooding. I could often see her olive-brown head poking out of the nest from time to time during this period. Even while she was in the process of laying her eggs, the Duchess would continue to improve the interior of her nest, lining it with soft fibers and the cottony willow fluff, milkweed fluff, and feathers. But once the eggs were all laid, she would remain on the nest for something like eleven to fourteen days until the eggs hatched—more or less. In fact no one knows for sure when the young actually hatch, since oriole nests are often high up in trees, and peering down inside the well-wrought *bolsas* would be difficult even at lower levels.

Once the young were hatched the Duke and the Duchess would work together to feed their hatchlings. Generally, one parent or the other would show up every ten or fifteen minutes at least, with a beak full of food. Soft-bodied caterpillars are said to be a favorite, as well as adult insects, including, in some instances, dragonflies. Orioles also eat soft fruits, and over the two weeks after hatching, as the young grew heavier and more feathered, the feeding would continue and the visits increase. Then, as the day of flight approached, the young would become more vocal and their chirps seemed to take on an urgency, thus evoking even more frenzy in the parents' feeding trips. Finally one day the young would appear—unattractive, greeny-olive things who would cling to the nest or squat on nearby limbs and crawl in and out of their nest, as if uncertain about the world beyond. And then by some alchemy known only to birds, the young orioles would come to believe that they can actually fly and take off, fluttering madly.

Over the next week or two I would see them around the yard, and the parents would continue to bring them food. And then, finally, by mid-July, the little family would disperse for parts unknown.

One afternoon after the fledglings had left, I was sitting in the garden watching the old gray, now somewhat ragged, nest sway with the limbs in the breezes coming in from the northwest. September was upon us; the Duke and the Duchess were gone; the swallows and the nighthawks had long since departed; the white-throated sparrows were showing up in the shrubbery and at the bird feeders, and blackbirds were beginning to form their big autumnal flocks.

In their wisdom, all the so-called neotropical migrants were heading home, leaving us alone to face a cold, bare season of discontent.

8.

The Ecology of the Potting Shed

Her mate devoured
by the cat, the cricket's wife
must be in mourning

❋ KIKAKU

Quite apart from the changes in habitat and pesticide use, there are other pressures on migratory birds. In fact, if you add up all the dangers, it is surprising that the class of birds has somehow managed to survive at all. Wind turbines and cell towers kill four to five million during migration. Millions collide with lighted buildings, as many as fifty million are hit by cars each year; birds are killed by oil spills, accidentally taken by fishermen, and millions crash into plate glass windows each year. On average, it is estimated that well over five hundred million birds die every year because of human causes.

One other of these dangers, one of the worst, can be found in my own backyard in the Vicarage Garden—*Felis domesticus*, the domestic house cat. The numbers vary, and it is not easy to estimate, but ornithologists have calculated that as many as one hundred million birds are killed every year by those innocent pets who lie abed most of the day, purring contentedly. The fact is, these gentle, seemingly benign, tame mammals are efficient predators of smaller creatures. One of the reasons they manage to spend so much time sleeping is that they have such skilled hunting abilities; they can attain their food without undue effort. That food includes insects, mice, rats, and voles, and also local birds.

In spite of these grim statistics, over the course of the thirty years in which the garden was in progress, I had three different cats. One I brought to the Swan Cottage where I lived when I first started the garden, but she died before I constructed the main house. After that, by way of consolation, I suppose, I was given two more by my ex-wife, who is forever rescuing cats and dogs and passing them on to friends and allies, or keeping them for herself.

These two were traditional tabby cats and were in residence when that other domestic animal arrived in their territory—the Jack Russell.

I should add that these two were not the only cats in the yard. Periodically, a local bobcat would pass though. I would often see his tracks in early and late winter, and other people on the compound saw him from time to time. Bobcats are actually more common in the region than is supposed. But they stay out of sight, and do not range through their territory to hunt. They simply select a good spot and wait. Their preferred prey, I am happy to say, is the cottontail rabbit, which so plagues the Vicarage Garden in certain years, but they will also eat mice and rats, and also birds and even insects.

As far as bobcats and birds are concerned, I always have to wonder about the fate of the young turkeys that are hatched somewhere in the woods near the garden and are regular visitors to the bird feeders of the compound. Some of them are so tame they are almost like barnyard chickens.

In any given year, a mama turkey will show up with a new brood of young, following loyally behind her. She usually arrives with six to eight poults, sometimes more. But slowly over the course of their first month, one by one, they disappear, so that in the end, only three or four will survive to adulthood. What eats them, no one knows. The fox population has been low in recent years, and I suspect that a mother bobcat has been helping herself to young turkeys and bringing them home to her little ones for dinner. Bobcats mate in late February or March, and the young are born in April or May, and are weaned just about the time the turkey chicks hatch, so the timing is right.

The other cat event was the presence, or more accurately the passage, of a mountain lion. These big cats, which are even more secretive than the bobcat, have a much wider range—as much as eighty square miles in some regions. Save for a subspecies known as the Florida panther, mountain lions are not supposed to be found east of the Mississippi. But tracker friends of mine have seen evidence of them in the large forested area in central Massachusetts, around Boston's Quabbin Reservoir, and another naturalist friend saw one jump across a trail in the same general area. One of the Scratch Flat hunters caught one in a night photograph triggered by an infrared camera, and I myself almost saw one on a June morning some years back.

Early on that particular morning I was down by the mailbox at the end of the driveway when I heard my daughter calling loudly to me from her house on the north side of the compound. She had just seen what she termed "a humongous" cat passing through her yard. She happens to be a trained field observer and knew exactly what the beast was, but, given the fact that she had a young child in her arms at the time, she was reluctant to quite believe it, let alone give chase. Having seen mountain lions in the West, she accurately noted all the field marks: pumpkin-shaped cat head, tawny color, long tail, and the classic cat stride.

I couldn't quite hear the details of whatever she was yelling about and turned to look up at her house. While I was turned away, the cat crossed the road, passing not twenty yards behind me.

I looked for tracks, but couldn't find any sign, although I heard later that someone in the sterile Quail Hollow Estates saw the tracks of a mountain lion—presumably the same one—about the same time.

I would like very much to have a resident mountain lion on Scratch Flat, if not in my actual garden, but the cats are rare in the Northeast, and in any case don't stay put.

Neither of my two thoroughly domesticated cats, I am happy to say, were bird eaters, in spite of the fact that they spent much of their time out in the garden. They lived on the property for over twenty years and never brought in a bird. That was not the case with mice, however. The aforesaid bodhisattva, contrary to his spiritual aura, was an efficient mouser. But oddly, he seemed to have a preference for catching snakes. He would periodically set off on a snake hunt in the morning and return at some point in late morning with his prey dangling from his jaws, voicing a low repeated and distinctive yowl unlike any of his other multiple vocalizations.

I was interested in this snake call, partly because he was the only cat I ever knew who favored snakes over birds and mice, but also because this habit got me wondering if cats have some form of as-yet-undiscovered primordial language. Recent studies of animal communication have uncovered the fact that vervets and other species of primates have certain calls for certain situations. Vervets, for example, have "words" for danger from above, in the form of eagles, and from below, in the form of leopards, and also a call for snakes. They would look up to watch for the eagle but not head for the trees if one of them gave the eagle call, but they would run for the trees with the leopard call, and they would stand up on their hind legs and look around in the grass if they heard their word for snake.

The cat's snake-catching ability also allowed me to hazard a rather general survey of the population of the snakes in the garden.

By far the cat's most frequent catch was a young garter snake. But he occasionally brought in other species, such as young milk snakes, and also the small brown snake, and once or twice, one of my favorites, the ringneck snake.

That garter snakes should be his most common catch was not surprising; they are the most obvious, but not necessarily the most common, snake in a typical garden—or at least a typical organic garden. Snakes, as well as toads, frogs, and salamanders, are sensitive to pesticides and can be sickened and killed by direct contact, or by absorption through their skin.

Garter snakes—named presumably for the decorative yellow and green stripes that resemble nineteenth-century garters—are resourceful hunters of garden pests such as slugs and caterpillars, although they will also eat garden allies, such as small toads and frogs. Almost every sunny day I see one or two in the garden as they flee for shelter under vegetation or into rock crevices. But even though they are the most evident snake, the brown snake is the most common, in spite of the fact that I rarely see them.

Brown snakes are small; the largest of them will grow to a foot at most, and they are a dull brown with a double row of black spots and a yellow to pink belly. They too are efficient hunters of garden pests, possibly even more beneficial than the garter snake, since there are so many of them. They tend to hide out under old boards, logs, rocks, and other sheltering spots, but I have seen them lying along the lower branches of my boxwoods from time to time, along with the small garter snakes, who seem to favor the upper levels of my hedges when the sun is shining.

There is probably no direct connection to all this snake interaction on my part and the cat's part, but it is interesting that years ago, when she was about six, one of the children wrote the first natural history of this garden in the form of a field guide. Her first entry in this tome was titled "The Snak." The text went on to describe the characteristics and habits of said snak—his narrow body, his cricket-eating habit, and the like.

Over the course of creating this garden, I have attempted to increase the habitat for the various reptiles and amphibians that are native to this region. For a few seasons, in order to get a better idea of the number of different salamanders that occur on the property, I left what are known as cover boards in likely spots around the grounds. These are short, eight by ten- or twelve-inch pine boards. Over time, salamanders will find them and shelter underneath, and in order to get a sense of what's around, you have but to lift the board. Most commonly, along with millipedes, sow bugs, and field crickets, I would find a red-backed salamander hiding under the boards, although I have also found the most handsome of the garden dwellers, the large, yellow-spotted salamander, an amphibian that includes some of my allies in its diet, such as crickets, worms, and spiders.

Years ago, a friend of mine rescued a nineteenth-century garden shed from destruction and figured—accurately—that it might make a nice addition to my garden. He somehow horsed the whole building up onto the back of his truck and together we unloaded it, and using log rollers dragged it down a garden path at the head of the driveway and set it in place. I subsequently transplanted some rhododendrons on either side and planted two willow trees to climb above it. My idea was to use it as a potting shed. But things never worked out that way and I ended up moving an antique chair into the building and using the place as a retreat—one of many around these grounds.

One of the reasons I like to have a few sheds, teahouses, and toolsheds around the garden is that they house various species of local wildlife. Phoebes came in a broken window of my newly acquired potting shed not a month after it was set in place, and in spite of the fact that they messed up the walls and floor with their droppings, I allowed them to raise a brood before I replaced the window and cleaned out the shed.

Paper wasps build nests inside the shed every year, and I generally let them stay too—they are slow-moving, easygoing wasps who are reluctant to sting. In fact, the males are sluggish, lazy creatures who cannot sting. If you can learn to tell the difference, you can even pick them up and kiss them, to entertain guests. The males have yellow faces and decurved antennae. The females have dark faces.

The shed also hosts a good population of jumping spiders, and at least four different web-building species that I have not been able to accurately identify, save that they appear to be in the genus of house spider. One year, a white-footed mouse had a fine mossy nest tucked in above one of the window frames. I used to take children to see her babies. She would dash out of the nest, run across the walls, and perch above a window under the old phoebe nest, and watch as I extracted one of her little pink mouse children to show to the human children.

Also in this shed, and in an old chicken coop I maintained for a while, I would find milk snakes. These handsome snakes have a pattern of reddish splotches on a gray background that vaguely resemble the patterns on venomous rattlesnakes and copperheads. Older country people here on Scratch Flat used to call them adders. I was warned one day by one of the local farmers to stay out of his fields, inasmuch as he had seen adders there. I questioned him on this and determined that he meant milk snakes.

The common name, "milk snake," comes from the fact that these snakes often inhabit cow barns, attracted there by the population of mice and rats—which are among their favorite prey species. Farmers assumed they were there to steal milk from their cows. These too are beneficial predators, although they will also take baby birds and eggs on occasion. Their usual fare, though, consists of mice.

There is a whole different microhabitat beneath the potting shed. The soil there is moist and cool in this section of the garden, and the building sits up on a foundation of rocks. Toads shelter from the heat of the day in the cool shade beneath, and if I cared to dig around in the wet ground below the foundation rocks, I am sure I could find a few red-backed salamanders.

The shed is cited close to a string of vernal pools that are located on Mr. Findlay's property to the northwest. He has two or three pools, and the drainage is generally east-southeast, so that the excess water runs under a stone wall in the so-called Wilderness of the Vicarage Garden and creates another vernal pool.

Although it is probably illegal, since you are not supposed to fool around with wetlands in this state, I have periodically tried to improve the pool slightly in order to encourage the wood frog and salamander populations here. I should clarify that the state wetland laws exist to keep wetlands from being destroyed by developers, whereas my alterations were intended to make sure they continued to exist and harbor local amphibian species. Nevertheless, I believe the law reads "alteration," and I presume that placing a few fallen tree trunks across the general drainage course in order to maintain a steady supply of water throughout the entire breeding cycle of frogs, toads, salamanders, and fairy shrimp counts as an alteration. But I dare not ask!

The presence of these vernal pools has meant that there is a fairly healthy local population of salamanders in the garden. Turn over any old log on the grounds that has been allowed to rot away in place and you can often find a red-backed salamander lurking. As with the common brown snake, these are rarely seen unless you go looking for them, but they are among the most common amphibians in the region and are easily recognized by their red backs and line of dark stripes along their backs. Ironically, this is one species of salamander that does not need water to breed. The females lay their eggs in the moist soil under rocks and logs and then stay with the eggs, guarding them, until they hatch. Other salamanders mate and lay their eggs in the vernal pools or shallow lake edges or ponds, and then move on, returning to their deep underground burrows for the rest of the year.

This group of so-called mole salamanders lead underground lives and are generally unseen for most of the year. But in late winter and early spring, as soon as the ground thaws, they leave their burrows and migrate en masse to vernal pools. Driving around the back roads of Scratch Flat on rainy nights in late March and early April is risky business for types like me, who care about salamanders and frogs. Thousands are killed on such nights—a major impact on some of the rarer species, since many of the vernal-pool breeding populations are already stressed because of rampant filling of these shallow ponds for new developments. Some, such as the blue-spotted salamander, are on the state endangered species list, and other mole salamander populations are being closely monitored in the state.

The blue-spotted, along with its relative the yellow-spotted, and the marbled salamander are beautiful, if rarely seen, amphibians. The blue-spotted spends most of its life unseen, underground, hunting worms and other invertebrates, and only comes out for a few weeks in spring. It is very rare and its very presence on a site slated for development has saved a host of less-threatened species of invertebrates—wood frogs, toads, nesting birds, voles, moles, and shrews, and all the associated shrubs, trees, and herbaceous plants and fungi on a given tract of land that would have been leveled and replaced with a house and a (no doubt) sterile lawn, parking lot, driveway, or road. We owe a lot to blue-spotted salamanders. To paraphrase Winston Churchill, never have so many species owed so much to so few.

Developers in this region hate them. The presence of one breeding colony of blue-spotted salamanders can hold up or even stop a multimillion-dollar scheme.

Periodically in spring I have found blue-spotted salamanders in the Vicarage Garden, although I have never found their egg masses in my own vernal pool. Presumably they arrived on the property from Mr. Findlay's ponds.

There is a state program that encourages landowners and interested parties to register vernal pools, in order to identify them so that they can be protected. The form to register the pools requires, among other things, the presence of what are known as "obligate species," which are essentially plants and animals associated with these types of wetlands, such as royal ferns. One year, having found a blue-spotted salamander in the yard, I determined to register my pool. I filled out the form, as required, included a photo of the salamander I had found, and—I thought—followed all the minute directions and sent in the form.

A letter came back a couple of weeks later stating that I had

failed to dot a certain *i* on the form and that I must redo it—
which I attempted. But by that time, the state had lost my original
photograph, so I had to wait for a year in order to catch another
blue-spot.

In the end I gave up. In any case, neither Mr. Findlay nor I, nor
anyone in or near the compound, would deign to fill a vernal pool,
so this little part of the world is safe.

9.

The Swan Cottage

I know a bank where the wild thyme blows,
Where oxlips and the nodding violet grows,
Quite over-canopied with luscious woodbine,
With sweet musk-roses and with eglantine . . .

❋ SHAKESPEARE,
A Midsummer Night's Dream

The summer of the wedding proceeded day by day. The rains ended in late June and the heat rose, a slow, hot desiccation with day after day of sun, the scent of morning flowers, the air filled with darting hoverflies, dragonflies, and swallows, and still, hot afternoons when nothing moved. Heat lightning flickered in the western skies, and we could hear the rumble of thunder, but no rain appeared. Day after day with no rain. The peonies were long gone by then, the tomatoes ripened; the yarrow and the daisy, the hawkweeds, and the Queen Anne's lace bloomed, and by mid-July the fireflies appeared and the crickets began to call. And then suddenly, it seemed, it was late August, and the wedding day was upon us.

The actual day dawned with a merciful freshness, and out in the garden, life marched on as it would any late-August day. The garden spiderwebs were jeweled with dew; the flies and bees buzzed in the hydrangea blossoms, the dragonflies awoke, dried their wings, and crisscrossed the open mead, alighting on flower heads to survey their next flight. The seed heads were ripening on the towering cosmos by this time, and goldfinches were riding the stems earthward as they landed and plucked the seeds.

By late afternoon the guests showed up in the garden in small leisurely groups. They helped themselves to drinks and wandered around the grounds, looking at trees and shrubs and chatting, until they were summoned to assemble in front of the Swan Cottage, where a cousin who had had himself ordained in some bizarre alternative religion, via the Internet, described to them the various "acts" of the wedding ceremony.

There was to be a traditional marriage procession in the style of ancient Greece, in which the wedding guests, who were provided with a variety of musical instruments, would march through the woods to a hemlock grove in Mr. Findlay's forest. Following the ceremony we were to exit in a recessional, led by the married couple. There would then be libations, and following that, the guests were invited to attend a masque, based on scenes from *A Midsummer Night's Dream*. After that, dinner.

The bride, a woman of original tastes, wore a voluminous, silky antique wedding dress with tiered layers of eyelet she had purchased at a local thrift shop. She wore white gardenias in her hair, and she carried a bouquet of goldenrods, New England asters, and wood ferns. In order to be in contact with her Mother Earth, she went to the altar, such as it was, barefooted. The groom outfitted himself in his father's ill-fitting tuxedo, and he too marched barefooted to his nuptials.

They claimed to be a very religious couple, but they weren't sure which religion, nor which god was in charge, so they wrote a ceremony that included as many religions of the world as they could dig up, including some extinct, primitive customs. There were three "priests," one representing the ancient Sumerian goddess Inanna, and the self-ordained cousin, plus some sort of generic forest being who appeared spontaneously. We never saw the forest spirit's face inasmuch as he wore a beaked mask in the Venetian style, complete with the feathers of exotic birds. The couple had insisted that the resident dog accompany them to the altar, so we outfitted him with a Superman cape belonging to one of the children and adorned his collar with wildflowers.

The altar consisted of a table covered in white linen, with a stuffed barred owl, two silver goblets, two silver candelabras, and a teddy bear. The goblets and the candelabras were vaguely Christian, and the owl was associated, perhaps, with the goddess Athena, but I never learned which religion the teddy bear was representing.

Led by a drummer, who sounded a slow, singular beat on an African djembe slung across his chest, we threaded our way along the woodland path, until we came to the place aforesaid by the master of ceremonies.

The bride was first married to a tree, a tradition adopted from one of the Indonesian island tribes. The idea was that if things went wrong, or if evil spirits attempted to enter into the couple's relationship, the tree would assume the hurt. The second, true marriage, would be protected from evil. For the tree marriage the bride was tied to one of the ancient hemlocks with a silken ribbon. Then, as we watched, the forest monster leaped out into the clearing, and as if spotting us for the first time, glared around at the assembled guests, turning his head sharply from side to side and up and down, reviewing us gorilla fashion. Then, concluding that we were innocent, he said—in English—"This is good! I welcome you."

He then proceeded to cut the bride free from her tree husband, whereupon she fled into the forest density, followed by the dog in his Superman cape.

At this point the groom appeared, only to find that his bride-to-be had disappeared. All this was part of some other obscure, perhaps extinct, religion, and it was the forest being who saved the day. He produced from his black robe a bullroarer, an ancient instrument used among tribal people the world around, but still prevalent among Australian aboriginal cultures. It was a flat stick attached to a long string, which he wheeled energetically around his head. The stick spun on its thong and soon a loud humming began to fill the air. The sound seemed to be everywhere and nowhere at once. It was, we learned later, the very voice of the forest, and the trick worked. Slowly, the bride emerged from her hiding place behind a stone wall, and approached the altar, where the groom stood waiting.

The priestess Inanna was there too, wrapped in ceremonial robes created from curtains and tablecloths, with a tea cozy as headpiece.

At this point, words selected from various sacred texts, including those from extinct religions, were read. The bride and groom uttered vows in a variety of languages, and then Inanna married them with a traditional exchange of rings, in the Western style.

Then, led by the high-stepping forest spirit and the newlyweds,

we danced out of the forest accompanied by cymbals and tambourines, and the cacophonous blaring of toy horns and whistles, the
dog prancing along with us.

The procession turned right in front of the Swan Cottage, and
followed a garden path along the western wall, then made a turn
around the circular *bosque sacré* and continued on to another circular path around a sundial, in the so-called Trellis Garden, then
down the allée of the trellis, under the grape arbor and the clematis and the climbing nasturtiums, to the mead, where we then
turned right again and entered the orchard. The happy throng
passed through the gate of the hornbeam wall, turned left, and
then left again in front of the teahouse, and danced down between
the flower beds, to the Lady Garden, all bright in that season with
the purples and reds and yellows and the blue carpet of creeping thyme. The horns still blaring and the cymbals and bells still
jangling, the group turned right again and proceeded through a
privet-lined path to the maze, which they entered and threaded
through. At the goal, the very center of the labyrinth, which is traditionally the entrance to the underworld, the bride and groom
halted and exchanged a second ceremonial kiss, which perhaps
went on a little too long for such a seriously religious wedding as
this.

Following this, the guests turned and walked out of the maze
and assembled in a cleared garden room behind the hornbeam
hedge for the masque. Then, with evening approaching, there were
champagne toasts, followed by an al fresco dinner.

※※※※※

I stumbled out into the summer garden the morning after the wedding party and wandered around the yard, dazed and half-nostalgic, remembering the events of the previous day and the evening festivities. Here, littering the mead, were overturned chairs, tables strewn with empty champagne bottles, forks and knives and pseudo-elegant plastic plates with spills of wine souring in the August morning sun and a few yellow jackets collecting around bits of leftover food, and honeybees investigating the icing of a remnant slice of the wedding cake.

The summer of the wedding was over. This was August 27th. The barn swallows were gone. On this day, somewhere above the garden, if I waited around in the fading light of dusk, I would hear a familiar nasal call and see nighthawks passing over the ridge of the drumlin on their way to Argentina for the winter.

I strolled around the flower beds at the edge of the mead, wandered down the trellis allée, and passed behind the wall of hornbeams to the teahouse. Someone had deserted a glass of champagne on the little wicker table in the teahouse, there were crumpled festive napkins on the couch, and a beautiful woman—I presume a beautiful woman—had left a gauzy silken scarf draped over one of the chairs. I picked it up and smelled champagne and a faint odor of roses.

I wandered on. On a bench just beyond the patch of turf, there was a toy horn, deserted there after the procession from the hemlock grove. I went down to the road through the privet allée beside the Bishop's Close to get the newspaper and stood there at the bottom of the drive, reading the headlines.

War again. A Christian army had swept into the deserts of

Arabia and clashed with the Saracens near Acre, just where some of the most vicious battles of the Crusades had taken place.

The market went up.

I walked up the driveway toward the house, passing the wall of shrubs and flowering trees along the north boundary. A few roses were still blooming beside the little ornamental bridge I had put in above the rivulet that runs along the wall from late winter to early summer. At the head of the drive, I looked up at the little potting shed at the end of the shrub-bounded allée. To the left was the Swan Cottage, the doors and windows flung open. Someone was sleeping there in the loft, and I had to stop and think for a minute which of the many guests at the various houses of the *ladou* that night were where.

Beyond the Swan Cottage lay the florid plantings of dogwood, rhododendron, pieris, rose of Sharon, hostas, plums, and, nearby, the laburnums, Japanese maples, Siberian pea trees, redbuds, and golden rain tree of the so-called *bosque sacré*. And guarding all this, beyond the western wall, was the dark forest where it had begun.

Looking back on the garden, and the recent events, and the fact that I have never considered myself a real gardener, much less a garden designer, I had to wonder: Where did it all begin, and how did it come to pass?

My earliest garden impressions were of the ruins of the gardens of the old estates and homesteads of the town in which I grew up, with their old trees, ragged privet hedges, overgrown frog ponds, and weedy garden rooms surrounded by tangled woods. This was my territory; we children were turned out into this world in the morning and not expected home until dark.

Near my own backyard, which was surrounded by old copper beech trees, there were two vegetable gardens of neighbors, one with a dank potting shed that offered a good hideout in a wide-ranging game we played endlessly known as Wolf, in which everyone would hide from a lone wolf who increased his or her pack by capturing hiders. The last captured was the winner.

Just across the road, on a hill above our house, was a brown-stone estate with grounds supposedly landscaped by the firm of Frederick Law Olmsted. The gardens here were maintained by a cruel Scottish gardener, cut in the style of farmer McGregor of *Peter Rabbit* fame, who would give chase if he caught you messing about on his grounds.

Later travels introduced me to the gardens of Europe, mainly the gardens of Italy, and in particular the Renaissance gardens taken over and reworked by English garden designers in the early nineteenth century and again in the early twentieth century.

All these and various American gardens slowly worked their way into the garden design that I eventually created. For better or worse.

But from a naturalist and environmentalist's point of view, I had to wonder whether all this garden work was justified. How can it possibly be ethical in an ecological sense to call in the timber operators and cut down a healthy forest of native trees that had grown in the place for over seventy-five years or so? And why should the tract of land that supplanted it be so lush with insects, snakes, toads, frogs, bird life, burrowing mammals, dragonflies, butterflies, hoverflies, wildflowers, and more than thirty-five species of flowering trees? White pines are native plants. The progression from an orchard of alien apple trees to a native forest is the natural order of things—the return of the native, so to speak.

The answer to this question, I learned, is complex.

Here in this section of North America, the earliest human settlers had developed a kind of controlled game-management in which they burned over sections of the forest to encourage the growth of blueberries and huckleberries. This in turn attracted the deer and the bear, which were staples of the primordial Native American diet. In Central and South America, the native people had already improved on this management. Among some Mayan cultures, for example, the natives encouraged semi-tame herds of deer and turkeys, which they slaughtered as needed. They also began to practice a form of horticulture in which they bred a family of grass that produced a tiny thumb-sized seed head into the universally popular food source known as corn.

This custom of altering nature to suit human needs began, it is believed, more than eight thousand years ago, and is not going to disappear as long as there are human beings left on earth—which, if things carry on as they are at present, may not be long, in terms of geological time. But in the interim, what about the rich biodiverse company of living things that share the planet with us?

My little experiment of cutting down a native stand of trees and replacing it with an artificial environment should have had the opposite effect of what actually happened. The biodiversity of wild things should have decreased. That, as the foregoing pages make clear, is not what happened.

White pines were originally an integral part of the mostly deciduous forest that eventually grew in this region after the ice retreated. The tree was part of the complex wilderness that the first European settlers saw when they moved into the territory in 1654. But the nature of those trees was far different from the relatively small white pines that now grow in this region.

Under natural conditions, the white pine was what is known as an emergent tree. They were everywhere in the landscape, but they grew singly, and they were very tall, and poked their feathery heads above the canopy of the surrounding forest of hickory, chestnut, oak, and maple that was the dominant forest type in this region. But after 1654 things began to change.

Most of these ancient, straight-stemmed giants were marked by the English with the King's broad arrow, a signature that indicated that they were "owned" by the King of England and were destined to become ships' masts. By 1800, most of these veteran pines were gone. And by 1830 more than 80 percent of the deciduous forest that once surrounded the pines was gone. By that time, the world here was all hayfields and orchards and extensive market gardens. Scratch Flat alone was a major producer of foodstuff. Beef, Hampshire pigs, apples, and vegetables supplied the nearby urban markets.

Starting in 1825, after the construction of the Erie Canal, things began to change again. The rich wheat fields of upstate New York were opened up, and over the next five decades farmers began the westward drift that would underlie the great Eurocentric expansion known as Manifest Destiny. Slowly, the New England agricultural fields were abandoned. First to go were the last ones cleared, mainly the hill towns of central New England. Hartland, Connecticut, for example, which lies in the foothills of the Berkshires, began losing its population in 1790 and continued to lose its residents until the late twentieth century. I lived in that town for three years in the middle of an eleven-thousand-acre state forest—all of it former agricultural lands; you could find well-fashioned stone walls there in the middle of nowhere.

Driving around the countryside in our time, you can still spot these past fields. If you look up at a distant hill slope and see a more or less square or rectangle plot of dark green you are probably looking at a former hayfield or pasture, now dominated by white pines. And therein lies part of the answer as to why my little acre-and-a-half plot of earth should outstrip a pine forest as far as biodiversity is concerned.

White pines are sun-loving trees. The ancient pines of this original biome grew as single trees, but after they were cut down and the forest around them was decimated by the agriculturalists of the eighteenth and nineteenth centuries, the seeds of the pines lay dormant in the earth. Furthermore, farmers often left a few white pine trees standing at pasture edges to offer shade to the grazing animals of the farmstead. Year after year, for as much as a century, these ancient veterans shed their seeds. As soon as the pasturelands were abandoned the seeds got their chance, sprouted, and made a dash for the sun.

The young trees grew vigorously and crowded in on each other, forming a dense canopy that shaded the ground and prevented any other vegetation from sprouting. Growth continued, and after forty or fifty years, the lower branches died off and the roofed net of branches continued to shed needles, thus creating, along with deep shade, a thick acidic duff of fallen needles and branches.

Here in the acidic soils and the darkness, only a few higher plants were able to grow, species such as wintergreen, starflowers, sarsaparilla, and partridgeberry.

This was the nature of the plot of land I encountered when I decided—as did my European forebears—to clear the forest and plant something else. Whether it was right to do so depends, I suppose, on which species you happen to be.

For Homo sapiens, such as the English Lady, it was a good thing. One can stroll at ease along grassy paths of the garden, among the saturated colors and scents of many varieties of flowering plants. This is also a good thing for many species of butterflies, and the ruby-throated hummingbird, the sole species of hummingbird that occurs in this region. It is also good for all the similar species of insects, birds, reptiles, and amphibians that currently enjoy this garden. But, to be fair, there are many species, such as sheep laurel, low-bush blueberry, starflower, lady's slipper, and the rare and elusive whorled pogonia, and birds such as the whip-poor-will, that a garden habitat such as mine is not good for. Furthermore, the white pine stand I cut down was part of a larger forest system that stretched from the agricultural lands of Scratch Flat, north-northwest, all the way up via corridors of forest, through New England, and on into Canada and the deep spruce fir forests of the Laurentian Shield.

All this comprises the largest continuous forest ecosystem in North America, outside the Pacific Northwest. And within these tracts of deeper forests, birds and mammals that do not live in garden-like ecosystems live and breed. Deep forest birds such as the veery and the wood thrush and wood warblers are found in such environments. The bobcat, and the fisher, moose, bears, and even the elusive mountain lion that occasionally wanders through, have returned to the region because of the deep shelter of the forest.

However, if you hike through these forests on a mountain trek, you could spend a whole day without ever seeing any of these larger mammals. And you might not see any of the birds, either, due to the thick leaf canopy, although you might hear them in spring. The same is true of the most biologically rich biome on earth, the tropical rainforest. Birds and monkeys, and the incredible array of air plants and orchids, and the diverse company of insects, are, for the most part, creatures of the canopy, and spend most of their time two hundred feet or more above the ground. The shaded forest floor seems strangely barren. You can hike for hours through a rainforest and remain completely oblivious of the diversity of life in these regions.

A garden, by contrast, is an altered environment, an "ecotone," in the words of ecologists. These are essentially disturbed areas on their way to becoming something else, which, in the northern tier of the American continent, is forest. The legend is that a squirrel could cross from the Atlantic coast to the Mississippi without ever touching the ground. This may not be entirely true; there were wide, grassy floodplains of rivers, and open beaver-created pastures and marshes, but the point is clear. There were a lot of trees.

In the edges between field and forest—the ecotone that a garden represents—you can experience even more density of species than you would in a single environment such as a forest or an open field. Growing in the Vicarage Garden are all the North American plants that I have assembled on this small plot of land, plus local alien species such as dandelions and hawkweeds that have come in on their own, plus ornamental and edible plants from Asia and the Continent and the subtropics that I grow there, and even tropical plants in the vegetable gardens. The garden is made up of the sort of vegetation that is found naturally in forests, and also in fields, and on mountaintops, in dry regions, and in tropical and subtropical forest. Quite an assemblage of plant species.

This, in the view of the strict native-plants-only gardeners who, to be true to form, should not grow so much as a tomato in their gardens, may not be the best of all possible worlds for all local species, or so the current argument goes. However, according to Jennifer Owen's book *The Ecology of a Garden*, in her little ecotone, certain local native species of insects and birds seemed to favor a few of her nonnative plants.

That may be true in Britain, but it is not necessarily true in North America. The argument against alien plants holds that the fruits of nonnative plants are not as nutritious as the natives, nor as attractive to herbivores as food plants.

Be that as it may, people are going to continue to plant the roses and peonies of Asian and Mideastern biomes, and cosmos and dahlias, which are native to Mexico, and rhododendrons, which thrive in the Himalayas, and hydrangeas and all the other Asian, African, and Australian and Pacific Island plants that collectors have been bringing to England and the Americas over the past two hundred years.

And it is clear that the birds and insects, mammals, reptiles and amphibians, and all the other vertebrates and invertebrates that inhabit my own little patch of the planet do not seem to mind.

In what is known to ecologists as a morphospecies survey, I once went around my grounds and counted only the number of clearly different types of plants or insects I could find. And in another general survey, I refined this method and counted the orders, families, and genera of plants and animals, without identifying the living things at the species level. Then I went through the gardens again, and counted the number of plants that I had brought onto the land, many of which were nonnative, although there were a good number of native species as well. Putting all this together, I eventually assembled a list of well over five hundred families and genera of plants and animals. Assuming a very conservative estimate of, say, four different species within these two broad taxonomic groupings, I estimated that over a thirty-year period, more than two thousand species of living things were surviving here—at least for a few years.

The time element is significant. A garden is an anthropocentric, artificial environment—it requires a gardener. If my grounds were abandoned for whatever reason, in the space of one growing season things would begin to change. The trees and shrubs I planted, the rhododendrons, ninebark, hydrangeas, boxwoods, along with the dogwoods, zelkova, katsura, stewartia, and Carolina snowbells, would carry on year by year and become part of the landscape, but there would no longer be any cosmos, or   nias, nor any other ornamental annual plants. The perennial.   ould slowly decline and the primal force of grass and nonnativ invasives such as bittersweet, multiflora rose, Japanese knotweed, and euonymus would take root and begin to spread. Slowly, in the second growing season, native plants such as the sun-loving birches, gray dogwood, and chokecherry would sprout in the mead and in those cleared areas where the invasive aliens had yet to gain a foothold. All these plants would grow higher over the next decade, until finally, wherever it could get in, the dominant plant that grew here when I first arrived—the ubiquitous white pine—would begin to outstrip them, shading out the shrubs and the shorter-lived small trees, such as the stewartias and laburnums.

In short, this garden is no more than a theater set for the little drama that was played out on a stage in my time. I may have had the ability to increase the biodiversity of the place—but only for a while. What will happen in the next act is unknown. But in that short match snap of time in which I worked this land we, all of us—people, plants, and wild and domestic animals—lived here in a little Eden of our own making.

EPILOGUE

The English Lady paid a visit shortly after the wedding, bringing with her a book by a famous neighbor of hers in Kent, Adam Nicolson, scion of the family that included his grandmother, the famous gardener Vita Sackville-West. Nicolson is now in residence at the family's estate, Sissinghurst, through an arrangement with the British National Trust, which has control of the house and the famous gardens on the property.

After the estate became part of the National Trust, Sissinghurst became a major tourist attraction, hosting tens of thousands of visitors each year who come to see Vita's famous white garden and the house and grounds that were so much a part of the story of the London-based Bloomsbury Group. The original working farm where Adam had played as a child back in the 1960s evolved into a sort of static museum of beautiful, but somehow sterile, flower beds.

After he took up residence at the estate, saddened by the loss of the original role that the working farm had played in the region, Nicolson began the task of restoring the farm and convincing the managers of the trust to grow the food to feed the visiting masses at its lunch rooms, and reinstate the place as an integral part of the original organic aspect of the local landscape.

The property was once a division of a larger section of Kent known as the Weald, which is the old Anglo-Saxon word for forest. In the fifteenth century, when Sissinghurst was built, the area was a patchwork of manor houses and farms set among low hills cut through with streams and winding lanes and tracks.

Some of that landscape still exists. I have visited there several times with the English Lady, and the land around Sissinghurst has narrow winding roads, wide valleys, low hills, and working farms. The Mole, of *The Wind in the Willows*, were he with us now, would much appreciate the plowed furrows and lanes of lingering evenings that can be found there—although, to be truthful, I daresay he could not have made it across any of the roads on a summer weekend, when half of London comes whining through in speedy little mole-killing cars.

Adam Nicolson's idea was to use Sissinghurst as a model farm for the surrounding region and establish, or reestablish, the Weald as a place in the metaphorical sense, a region with an identity and a deep history.

The English Lady had arrived at our house in early September, and since I had spent so much effort on flower beds and the like that summer, I had not paid much attention to my vegetable plots. As a result, she and I would make the rounds of the two local farms for produce.

Lady Theodosia was most impressed with Scratch Flat, or at least that part of the tract that still maintains working farms, the three farm stands, and the wooded hills to the northeast.

"Nothing like the Weald, mind you, but rather pleasing in an American sort of way," she said.

She was quite right in this assessment. Scratch Flat has a county road running through it, and nowadays only a small part of it is still in agriculture.

All this talk of saving farms and whole landscapes got me thinking more about the town in which Scratch Flat is located. The assemblage of plants and animals in my garden, in comparison with the current and apparent future state of agriculture and suburban properties in the town, made me consider the role of a garden as a part of the ecological fabric of a town or region.

I had been rereading Jennifer Owen's book *The Ecology of a Garden* at the time, which further engaged me in my thinking about gardens and local landscapes. Owen's book has a photo of her property, which, as she states, is not so different from any other cottage garden of the tens of thousands that are strewn over England's fair and pleasant land. Elsewhere in her book she poses a question: Are suburban gardens England's most important nature reserves?

Such environments are now so common as to represent an ecological habitat on their own, and unlike less managed lands, such as forests, floodplains, heathlands, and meadows, which are under threats of one sort or another, suburban and exurban yards are increasing. If these lands could be managed in such a way so as to maintain and even increase local species of plants and animals, development as such might not be as detrimental to the environment as is generally supposed.

Although the particular community around Scratch Flat has managed to preserve a certain amount of wild open space and has more working farms than most towns in the region, the general direction is toward more development, more traffic, more hard-topped parking lots and buildings, and probably more developments in the style of the nearby Quail Hollow Estates, with its monocultural landscape and its climate-controlled environment and surfeit of electronic entertainments.

Presuming that energy supplies of one sort or another manage to endure, and the human population continues to expand, development seems to be a fact of life. But what if the model of the Vicarage Garden were replicated all across Scratch Flat or even the town as a whole? How would one accomplish such a thing?

First, of course, would be to preserve the last two working farms of Scratch Flat. Together these two agricultural tracts grow a huge amount of produce, as well as eggs, poultry, lamb, beef, and pork, although no longer any dairy products, nor any fruit. Both these farms have substantial areas of woodland as well, and as I have pointed out, these woodlands, which are in both private and public holdings, extend in various corridors and interconnected patches all the way up to Canada and the wild boreal forests of the Laurentian Shield.

Secondly, I began making big plans for my erstwhile wife's small field across the road from the Vicarage Garden. She had already cleared the tract, which consisted mainly of multiflora rose, burning bush, and other invasive plants, and replanted the area with meadow grasses.

Just east of her cleared field there was a strip of woods with a fine stand of white birch at the edge, and I thought to get in there and clear out all the invasives and replant or restore the area with native wild plants. That done, I would see to leasing out, or grant outright, the open field, to grow produce.

The other potential prospect in my probably unrealistic fantasy was a twenty-seven-acre parcel of land that lies just east of my ex-wife's field and runs down to the banks of the nearby Beaver Brook, a property now under the control of a local sportsmen's club. The woods here consist mainly of the dreaded white pines that characterize the west side of the drumlin, but the tract has some interesting geological anomalies, including the ridge of wind-blown sand dunes created after the glacier retreated from the region. The forest itself does not have the diversity—or at least not the same ecological makeup—of the farms and my garden and the two gardens and plant collections of my neighbors. By contrast, the nearby floodplain of the wide, north-running stream is biologically diverse. Marsh wrens, bitterns, the occasional sora rail, and the usual assortment of marsh birds such as herons, wood and black ducks, as well as three turtle species, water snakes, and pickerel frogs, green frogs, and bullfrogs all find food and shelter there. There may also be a population of the increasingly rare leopard frog in among the dense grasses and pools, as well as the locally threatened Blanding's turtle. Otters, beavers, and muskrats also live there. In fact the marsh is already listed on records as one of the most biologically diverse areas in the state.

At the end of a track leading from the sportsmen's clubhouse to the brook there is a high and dry grassy bank where the brook takes a wide westward bend and runs along the shore. The rest of the stream is surrounded by wide cattail marsh and buttonbush, and can only be reached by the two bridges that cross the brook, one at the southern end and one in the north, just before the stream debouches into a local lake. The high bank provides perfect access for canoes or kayaks. In my wildest dreams, I see the club opening to the public as the renamed Beaver Brook Boating

Club, complete with a launch site at the high bank and walking trails that would connect with other wooded trails that already run along the east and west side of the floodplain of the brook.

I could also imagine a footbridge crossing over to a new commercial shopping development that has preserved some of the property as open space with educational signs and nature trails, and has been working to eliminate invasive plants from the land.

The other impossible dream would be to remake the yards and gardens of the Quail Hollow Estates—tear out the lawns and plant vegetable gardens, and landscape the properties with a wide variety of trees, shrubs, and herbaceous plants instead of the repeated uniform plantings of Norway maple, blue spruce, and rhododendrons with no weeds to speak of and a deathly ground cover of red-dyed wood chips and sterile lawns and all of it maintained with chemical fertilizers and pesticides.

And why stop there? Development is fast approaching this formerly rural community, and there is within the town a small, generally unheralded group of citizens who cry out for preservation of the farms and open space and support of local foods. The fastest-growing sector of American agriculture is now what is known as periagricultural; that is, farms within a thirty-five mile radius of an urban center. This agricultural economy has been vastly underestimated in the previous analyses, and has now been updated and generates some $4.8 billion in local revenues. Just what a financially hard-pressed community with arable land could use.

The local community fits this description perfectly. It is located thirty-five miles from a major urban center and still has a lot of arable land, although not all of it actively farmed. And yet the great lumbering beast of government is slow to learn and slower still to act. The idea that growing food locally is economically viable and will be even more so in the future, is still considered a radical flight of the imagination. Nonetheless, in the face of this, the more enlightened voters fight on to save what they can under the current democratic system.

Were I the Lord of the Manor, in the style of the original family that held Sissinghurst in the fifteenth century, I could simply decree that all woods and farms beyond the core of the village shall be preserved as they are in perpetuity, that all wild plants and animals shall be respected, that the farms shall remain small and family-owned, and managed organically, and that all excess foodstuffs produced thereon shall be distributed equally and free of charge to the more hard-pressed members of the local peasantry.

But alas, I am but the groundskeeper of a modest garden and lord of nothing save my own two-acre kingdom and its citizen plants and animals. In the end, the dream fades, reality creeps in, and to be more pragmatic, it may be best to teach by example and simply stay home and cultivate my garden.